KNOWN & LOVED

by

DAVE COLLINS

Without limiting the rights under copyright reserved below, no part of this publication may be reproduced, stored in or introduced into a retrieval system, or transmitted, in any form, or by any means (electronic, mechanical, photocopying, recording, or otherwise), without the prior written permission of both the copyright owner and the publisher of this book.

Published by BLACK CREEK PUBLISHING GROUP
2102 Kimberton #266
Kimberton, Pa. 19442

www.blackcreekpublishinggroup.com

Copyright © 2013 Dave Collins

All rights reserved.

ISBN: 0989532364
ISBN-13: 978-0-9895323-6-5

LCCN: 2013948807

KNOWN & LOVED

DEDICATED TO:

Sharon

Kayla and Nathan

Brenna

Chance

Aaron and Elizabeth

Tanner

Avery

Rylan

DAVE COLLINS

CONTENTS

	Acknowledgments	Pg 7
1	The Centrality of Relationships	Pg 13
2	The Duplicity of Being Known	Pg 33
3	Delving Into the Depths of a Soul	Pg 47
4	Love – The Ultimate Choice	Pg 61
5	Snapshots of Love Done Well	Pg 75
6	Lost & We Don't Know It	Pg 89
7	The Weakening of Relationships	Pg 111
8	God's Provision to Restore Relationship	Pg 121
9	The Connection – God Knows Us	Pg 155
10	Jesus – Our Example	Pg 179
11	Knowing & Loving God	Pg 195
12	Knowing & Loving Myself	Pg 211
13	Knowing & Loving Others	Pg 237
	Notes	Pg 249

DAVE COLLINS

ACKNOWLEDGMENTS

It has been several years since the day Cheryl Fletcher and I were in the Young Life office in Austin, discussing different things we were studying in the scriptures. I do not remember the year, but I remember the discussion about being known and being loved. That night I went to bed, but could not sleep. I could not get our discussion out of my mind. I stayed up all night outlining the book you have before you now. I told Cheryl I was going to write this book, but would give her credit for the idea. So Cheryl, here it is. If people hate it, can I blame you?

I felt called by the Lord to write this, but must admit I let a number of things get in the way of completing the project. Some were pretty significant and legitimate, others were just excuses. I would like to thank Jim Lieto and Jack Lesch for pushing me to finish the project. Thanks guys. I appreciate our relationship. It's what this book is all about. You do life well.

Peter, Lamar, Aaron, Sharon, Galen, and Buc......thanks for reading the early manuscript, and offering your insights. I give you credit for helping me with clarity of expression and making this something people will want to read. Lamar, I really treasure those Saturday mornings we spent editing and reworking the ideas expressed here. What a great friend you have been! Thanks.

Thank you Anna and Alex for allowing me to share your story. You are a great example of love lived out. Thanks for letting others know you. I may be a putz, but I am blessed with good friends like you who know how to love. My life is better because of our relationship.

Dan, without your insight and experience with the Waorani,

I could not have told their story with clarity and passion. Thank you for your friendship, and for sharing your experience and understanding of these people with me. I'm waiting to see what God does with us next.

What a story we can tell about Judy Henry my high school friend, and now, my publisher, editor, and whip cracker! Who could have guessed you would publish my book at this stage in our lives? I love the fact we were able to meet each other again. I am the beneficiary of your wisdom and insight. I appreciate your partnership in this project, how generous you have been in many ways, and your commitment to do all you could to make this project the best it could be. I look forward to our next project.

Thinking about all the great friends I have had in Young Life, it would be hard to imagine anyone taking your place to teach me so many of these concepts. I feel like I have hundreds of "kids." You may not be mine biologically, but my family is large. We have loved each other, and I relish the privilege of soaking up all the time I can get with many of you who have grown up. Those with whom I have worked modeled for me many of the principles expressed in these pages. You continue to make my life full.

Kayla and Aaron, you know I love you deeply. Now a whole lot more people can see that in print. Thanks for your patience with a father who stumbled through your early years. You are the best kids a father could have. I'm so proud to be your dad.

Sharon, you have been more patient than anyone with me. You have loved me deeply, and supported me for over 40 years in every way. I have been blessed beyond words. You are a gift to me. I can't wait to see what our next years will look like. I hope I have learned enough to give you all the

KNOWN & LOVED

love you deserve for all the years we have left together.

DAVE COLLINS

IT IS NOT GOOD FOR MAN TO BE ALONE.

God

… DAVE COLLINS

1

THE CENTRALITY OF RELATIONSHIPS

Children are great teachers. Part of my education began with the question, "So, Aaron, how did you like the club?"

"It was ok." He answered with the typical minimal adolescent response.

"Well, tell me how different was it from what you do at school? Did you like it? Which did you like the best?"

"To tell you the truth, I like the weights at school a lot better. I like the free weights. They seem to be better. The machines make it easier, because you don't have to balance the weight as you lift it. They don't do as much good with the same weight. Besides, I felt funny. Everyone was like you. They were older, and they all seemed to be in their own little world. I like lifting with my friends. It's more fun to do it with them. We mess around and have fun when we aren't spotting or lifting."

My son, Aaron, was a freshman in high school at the time, and enjoyed all kinds of sports. His favorite was football, and he went through all the extra effort needed to excel in the sport. Included in his regimen was weight lifting. Over the Christmas holidays, Aaron was worried about losing some of the strength he had gained since starting the off-season lifting program. I offered to take him to the local health facility where I work out. Aaron had been inquiring about my own efforts to stay in shape, and the kind of facilities in which I worked. (I think he was questioning the effectiveness of the program.) The opportunity to work out with me was greeted with enthusiasm.

Aaron liked the looks of the club. As we worked our way toward the weight room, he said he also liked the looks of the pool and dressing room. Since my routine involved both aerobic and strength exercises, I started my routine on the stationary bicycles. Aaron was not interested, and went straight to the weight machines located in three rows down the middle of the room. I watched him move from station to station, and eventually joined him as I finished my workout. Our conversation began after we had showered and started back home.

Aaron's response to my question was a revealing statement. His evaluation of a fine health club was based primarily in relational terms. Though he did prefer free weights, he chose to work with machines at the club. There were free weights in the same room with top-of-the-line benches, dumbbells, and other free weight apparatus. However, he would have had to work out with people he did not know. He felt awkward and uncomfortable, lifting with strangers. Rather than take that risk, he chose to work on the machines he considered inferior.

His evaluation of the club members present was accurate. Businessmen and housewives are the primary patrons of my club. Our goal is to squeeze in short workouts every week in an attempt to maintain some standard of physical fitness, retain youthfulness, or maintain a degree of physical attractiveness. Most of the men work out alone. They, like me, have a specific routine that can be completed within a specific time span. There is little interaction and conversation other than between a few who schedule their workouts with a friend, or those who choose to work with a trainer.

Aaron's friends, those fellow members of the football team, were an integral part of his weight lifting experience. The relationships, and time spent in the development of those relationships, played a key role in the experience. They had a common goal to gain strength and skills in order to have a winning football team next year. They spoke a common language centered on common interests, and shared in each other's lives. Mutual friendships developed during routine activities of a high school student's life provided plenty of experiences to laugh and dialogue about. He and his friends complained about the hard workouts, and the drills the coaches ran the team through. Aaron often brought the conversation home talking about hard workouts, mat drills, and wrestling competitions. It seems pain and exhaustion is easier to bear when it is shared. Shared joy is joy enhanced. Any activity done with others has more meaning. Even the most adventurous and exciting experiences pale in comparison to those done alone. Life is meant to be shared. We humans are designed for relationship.

I think what Aaron may have been feeling was something like watching a college football game on a business trip – alone. It would not be one's alma mater, but a team playing an exciting game in the crisp fall air before 50,000 screaming fans. One would experience the same sensory stimuli, the smell of fast food, the jostling of the crowds, the deafening roar of rabid fans, and school bands playing familiar marches to pump up their team. You would feel the electricity of the students, and see the progress of the game itself, but something would be missing.

It is not done that way. We go to see teams we know. We want to participate in the game by feeling a connection to one of the teams. We want a sense of belonging with the throngs of people cheering for their boys, and we usually attend with a friend. Aaron participated with me in a sterile environment; involving the kind of physical activity, he loved doing with his own buddies, in their own place, and for their own purpose. Even though I was there, it was the kind of activity he preferred doing with his friends. Relationships form the center of life. Any undertaking, any accomplishment, any experience, will have more meaning if it is shared with a friend. As I write now, I am searching the far reaches of memory trying to recall the earliest experiences of my youth. I am recalling the most exhilarating moments, the times I felt fulfilled, scared, content, overwhelmed by beauty or ugliness.

I remember my earliest Christmas as a young child bundled snugly in blankets and quilts stuffed in the big family chair in the living room. Excitement and laughter filled the room as people milled around the brightly lit Christmas tree in front of the chair. My mom gave me a big yellow toy truck and put it on my lap. I could not move my arms to play with it; they were tucked so tightly in the blankets. I was fortunate to be able to participate in the Christmas festivities, because I had pneumonia and was not permitted to do much. I remember very little about that Christmas, except the sense of being cared for and loved. The family knew I would feel better, and they gave me a great toy. They tucked me in, and cared for me. It is a sweet memory because of the people involved. It was not the fact it was Christmas, or that I loved the truck so much. I loved the people.

I remember an older friend, Randy, who did everything with me in my pre-school and elementary years. We climbed trees, fished, and hiked in the woods near our house. Randy was there when I fell out of a tree, and had the wind knocked out of me. It was Randy who claimed he was more of a man than me. We settled the case by betting on who could walk further on freshly poured asphalt. We blistered our feet together that day. In junior high and high school, football and track dominated my life. There were some personal accomplishments, and recognition achieved through those sports. There was a tremendous sense of joy and fulfillment, but as I try to focus on a great play or event, faces come to mind and drive the events to the background. It is the people I remember. As I mentally scan the experiences of my life, whether good or bad, this fact remains constant. Relationships are the subject matter of the mosaic of my life. They are also the frames. They are the light and shadows. Is it not so, with all human existence?

This brings me to a question. Why? Why is it that, try as I might, I cannot remember anything without a person being somewhere involved, and why are my memories defined by those people? Why is it, when I remember my first car a red 1958 Volkswagen bug affectionately called "the apple", I remember the time I took a date in it without the front passenger seat? The defining thought of "the apple" was a strange and wonderful evening with a girl in high school, not the value of the car itself. "The apple" gave me freedom and a sense of significance. It provided a means to get a job, and make money. It was the first thing of any value I ever owned. There have been other "things" in my life that I expended excessive energies to achieve or acquire. At the time, they seemed indispensable and necessary, but shrink in relevance to the power of relationship.

We fall prey to the error in thinking that things, achievements, or personal experience can meet all the needs of life. Perhaps the answer to why people define memories lies in the nature of life, in the fact that humans are not inanimate. It seems we humans are more than mannequins built to display the latest trend or the hottest new fashion. There is something about us that is meant to be known and that deserves to be loved.

Some years ago, someone with an entrepreneurial spirit developed a grand promotional scheme. The idea caught on making its developer a great deal of money. The idea was "pet rocks." In its promotion, they professed, everyone needed one. They were easy to keep, were low maintenance, and never wandered off. There was no need to put up fences, invest in veterinary medicine, or pet food. Fortunately, the fad passed quickly due to the flaw in the gimmick. An inanimate rock had none of the qualities usually sought after in a pet. Inanimate objects do not relate to living beings, so the joke soon lost its punch. Rocks, once more, resumed their role as things to skip across water, obstacles to dull lawnmower blades, and objects used to prevent papers from being blown away. Even though we can laugh at the pet rock phenomenon now, the subtle error of using inanimate objects as a means of touching our lives was inherently unfulfilling. Inanimate objects, serving as a substitute for a genuine relationship, will not satisfy. We may fall for the idea that seeing, tasting, or touching something will meet our deepest emotional need for love, or that sensory pleasure can replace or satisfy as well as love. We fail to recognize the built in emotional and spiritual needs all people possess. We are spiritual beings just as much as we are physical beings. There is a reason for our existence, going beyond ourselves, that can only be discovered by knowing one another on a different level. Having more things than someone else does not prove our value, or our reason for existence. It is a false measure of self-worth. Neither fame nor power, satisfy the need for pure relationship. The recognition they potentially deliver can never match the impact love and respect provide in a good relationship. Sometimes, we submit to the idea these substitutes will satisfy, only to discover an emptiness we cannot quite put our finger on. Likewise, it is an illusion to think the pleasure produced by our sensory organs can meet our emotional and spiritual needs as well as relationships.

The human sensory organs have incredible power to convey pleasure. Furthermore, the pleasure felt can be so overwhelming as to become addictive. The argument is not whether inanimate objects affect humans or can have a strong bearing on the quality of existence. They simply cannot match the power of one life touching another. The problem is their power is limited to the physical realm. Often men and women seek to ease emotional burdens by means of inanimate objects or substances. Persons become dependent on the physical pleasure afforded by the relational substitute, while never having the emotional need met. Even worse, the emotional need is heightened as it is starved in the obsessive search for fulfillment. A greater obsession to meet the hungering need can develop. Emptiness and difficulties arise when one seeks emotional satisfaction with what can only produce momentary physical pleasure. People are seeking, at an alarming rate, to meet emotional needs through physical objectives in our culture. The examples are obvious. Drugs, food, materialism, and sex are abused at all levels of society, by all ages, and by both sexes. When I speak of sex, I am referring to the physical, sexual, relationship without the underpinning commitment of marriage. It is the one-night-stand sex indulged on a casual basis for momentary pleasure.

I know a young woman who grew up in a home where relationships were sterile and cold. Her father was present physically, but did not seek to know her. He did not seek to know her thoughts or touch her emotions. All was well, if she behaved and was a good girl. She functioned well, as long as she could perform and receive the praises of those around her. However, her emotional starvation often rendered praise and accomplishments empty and shallow. When she was under stress to perform, or feeling the need for emotional involvement, she discovered pleasure of the palate took her mind off the stress. Over years, the pleasurable sensation found in food has been a salve during times of stress and the need to be touched emotionally. The result has been a struggle to maintain reasonable weight. She finds herself thinking about food at inappropriate times, and has a deep dissatisfaction within herself about her figure. A tension exists between the desire to eat, and the desire to look good and maintain her weight. She does not like to look in the mirror. It is becoming obvious to her, that tension has not gone away, and eating only intensifies her anxiety.

Volumes have been written about the dangers associated with drug abuse. Drugs, as a means of relieving emotional tension, only dull the emotional pain for a period of time. They do not resolve the problem behind the pain and in the end destroy lives. Sexual addictions are on the incline. The deterioration of families, loss of understanding about commitment, and widespread increased strains of sexually transmitted diseases have been the result of sexual freedom and experimentation. It is obvious; the pleasures of casual sex have not produced emotional satisfaction. The results have increased both emotional and physical pain in our society. Beside the fact sensory stimulation fails to touch our emotional needs, I find in cases where physical and visual stimulation are used as a means of achieving pleasure, certain laws are in effect.

PHYSICAL PLEASURE IS SHORT LIVED

Nerve endings respond to sensations. They transmit the sensation to the brain where it is interpreted as being pleasurable or otherwise. As long as the nerves receive stimulation, the brain has data with which to interact and interpret. When the sensations terminate, the brain moves on to other functions.

For example, seated at a table in a well-known restaurant is a businessman we will call William. He stopped in the restaurant before going to his hotel for the night. He notices the ambiance of the finely decorated room, the enticing aromas, and the anticipation of a tasty meal. He will enjoy his dinner, and perhaps remember this as a good place to eat. However, the meal will soon be forgotten. His nerve endings received the data. His brain interpreted the data concluding the food was good. The evening ended, and was forgotten.

PHYSICAL STIMULATION MUST BE REPEATED

When one encounters physical stimulation that has been interpreted as pleasurable, the mind stores the data. Should that person have an opportunity to experience the pleasure again, the mind will signal to "go for it." Even the thought of the experience is enough to send the signal. Since the mind can only interpret the signals received by the nerves, it cannot reproduce the sensation. It can only recall the memory of the sensation. When William returns to the city of the famous restaurant, his mind will recall the former experience perhaps causing him to choose to return for another meal. The memory alone will not produce pleasure. It only acts as a stimulus. Therefore, to feel pleasure, the act must be repeated physically. Positive reinforcement creates a drive to repeat pleasurable acts.

PLEASURE CONTAINS A LAW OF DIMINISHING RETURNS.

The interpretation of sensation derived from an initial encounter produces a standard in the mind from which all future encounters are measured. Somehow, repetition produces less sensation, and a new experience may completely overwhelm the former sense of pleasure.

William may experience decreasing enjoyment, if he returns to the same restaurant every time his travels take him to that city. A good place to eat becomes just another stop.

From personal experience, I recall the trauma and euphoria of my first date. With hands moist with perspiration, and after what seemed to be an eternity, I finally held her hand. All traumas blew away in ebullient euphoria. I got pretty good at holding hands. My hands quit sweating. It became a casual thing. But, holding her hand lost its power when my girlfriend's lips first touched mine. Holding her hand was nice, but it held nothing in comparison to that first kiss. As my dating experience grew, I always enjoyed holding hands, but a kiss was what I anticipated. For those who experience the ultimate physical intimacy without the corresponding emotional commitment in marriage, even the act of intercourse will lose its height of pleasure through repetition.

Life can become frustrating and hold a vague sense of emptiness, if pleasure seeking is the driving force. One solution to the dilemma created by the emptiness is to seek fresh activities to produce maximum potential pleasure. A trial and error system of life can develop, as new experiences are sought after. The mind compares the pleasure achieved with each new experience. Those that rate highest are repeated; until the pleasure produced is reduced to such a point, it becomes a source of frustration. Life becomes a never-ending search for new activities to replace worn out pleasures and elusive sensory fulfillment.

Some find pleasure in shopping, and buying new things. The advertising industry capitalizes on the fallacy that things give emotional pleasure. They promote products with the slogan "you need this, you will be a better person with this, your friends and acquaintances will recognize your achievements if you have this." In the American culture, character is often judged by appearance rather than quality. There is a t-shirt describing this philosophy. "The one who dies with the most toys is the winner." Unfortunately, the newness wears off all new toys. The luster vanishes, and the need for change repeats itself. Increasing technology makes everything obsolete quickly. Someone is always getting the newest item prompting another to keep up. Things break and financial resources are limited. Materialism, in the end, only adds tension to life. It cannot give life.

An increasing number of people have opted for the pleasure seeking treadmill, crowding their lives with multiple activities often at a frenetic pace. Thrill seeking and dangerous "extreme sports" have become very popular. Sexual freedom has led to a new phenomenon called "friends with benefits" or "hooking up." They have filled their lives with things and activities. Yet, a deep sense of peace and fulfillment remain elusive. People have failed to take the soul into account. It is in the hidden regions of the soul where relationships leave their mark.

At a restaurant next to our former example, William the businessman, was seated a young couple on a romantic date. A meal was placed before the pair while soft music created a warm mood. Through the filtered lights, one can see that special look in the eyes of each. The aromatic fragrance wafted above the table enveloping the couple as their meal was presented in wonderful colors and patterns stimulating their appetite. An explosion of flavor filled their palate with the first bite. Time stopped as two lovers slowly shared a meal together.

I could be writing about my wife and myself. While we attended the University of Houston, we often went to a little Italian restaurant down the street from the main campus. We walked there during the day, or would go in the evening. This small frame house became a romantic getaway for college students. Walls had been knocked down, and archways formed between rooms. Ivy hung around the heavily shaded windows, and wonderful murals were painted on various walls depicting life in Italy. They hung enlarged photographs of many famous locations in antique looking frames. The smells from the kitchen, barely a few feet away from any table in the house, sweetened the rooms with the enticing aromas of freshly baked bread, tomatoes, and garlic. The owners were Italian and filled their restaurant with a hominess born of a natural love for their homeland and their food. I have never been able to find any restaurant in forty years that could match their lasagna and garlic bread. I suspect this failure is more due to the fact my wife and I are no longer in the early stages of love. Can you feel the nostalgia in my lengthy description of a simple restaurant?

My visits to restaurants have now taken on the characteristics of the businessman. While the man seated at the table in the corner partook of a wonderful meal, he was more likely in deep thought about his agenda for the following day than taking in the sensory pleasures of his meal. That couple for years to come may return to the same restaurant, and recommend it to their friends. Contemplating our scene at the restaurant, we might ask the question, "Why did the meal have more meaningful emotional pleasure for the couple rather than the businessman? Why did they remember every detail of the evening even as the memory faded in the mind of the other patron?"

The answer lies in the nature of humanity. We are more than physical beings; more than a mass of electrical impulses passed along cellular conduits, more than cause and effect or learned responses influenced by positive and negative feedback. Our physical selves must also interact with an unseen soul and spirit. Furthermore, we believe there is a hierarchy of importance between our physical and our unseen selves. I believe our physical nature is most basic. It provides a dwelling place for the soul and spirit, requires upkeep and maintenance, and provides a setting in which the soul can interact with life on an emotional and feeling level. The body and soul work with the spirit to deal with the ultimate questions of life....purpose, meaning, and our place in the universe.

The concept of humanity functioning out of a hierarchy of values is not a new idea. A.H. Maslow, a humanistic psychologist, developed a theory called the hierarchy of needs. Basic to his theory are the presuppositions that man is capable from within himself to function in a fully healthy manner, understand himself and his place in the cosmos, and achieve completeness in life. He felt five needs as they were met in adequate degrees acted in a stair step fashion in the development of exceptional human beings. The lower needs were more basic and easily met. These he called the physiological needs including adequate food, water, and basic requirements for existence. As these were met, the need for safety emerged. Safety involves structure, security, and predictability. Having physiological and safety needs met created the drive to have intimacy, to belong, and to be loved. With the sense of belonging intact, Maslow felt a person was driven to feel esteem. The esteem essentials include prestige, acceptance, status, and self-esteem. Finally, a person was driven to achieve self-actualization. This need is a sense of destiny and completeness within himself. He felt few achieved this latter state.

Though I disagree with Maslow's presuppositions, I find his basic hierarchy interesting. He describes one as driven to achieve more as each need is met. I observe that men and women are not satisfied with food and shelter. They do exhibit the desire to belong, and be recognized. They seek to understand the reason for life, and personal existence. If physical elements were satisfying, men and women would not be driven to achieve more. We humans are more complex than that. There is something unseen inside us craving attention. Humans seem to indicate a hierarchical makeup. I propose a hierarchy based on physical needs, soul needs, and spiritual needs.

It is obvious that we are physical beings. If we fail to put food and water in our bodies, they will weaken and die. Basic physical necessities must be met. However, body and soul stand together. They are both intertwined and interactive. Each is affected by the other, and cannot act independently. Those who are physically ill focus their attention on physical recovery. Emotions may be drastically altered, sometimes leading to depression or even suicide. One of the reasons I joined a health club was the realization that my emotional state of mind is closely tied to my physical condition. When I work out, increasing strength and cardiovascular condition, I have more physical energy throughout the day, and I am more positive and robust emotionally. I enjoy people more. I enjoy life more. In the same way, our physical bodies can be affected by our emotions.

There was a period when my wife and I were dating, when she felt we should break up. I was already in love with her at the time. Emotionally, I was hit hard when she ended our relationship. For some time, I noticed a lack of energy. I did not feel well, and did not eat well. A person's spiritual state will likewise affect his outlook on life. One's spiritual perspective is a source of hope, or dread. It affects ones emotions and sense of wellbeing. I have been amazed in studying the life of William Carey, Hudson Taylor, Abraham Lincoln and other noteworthy individuals. They have faced seemingly insurmountable obstacles. They have faced death. They have faced the loss of loved ones. Yet they each had hope and endurance. They had a sense of purpose and wellbeing.

In contrast to these encouraging examples of men and women who lived an amplified version of life overcoming great odds, I have observed a group of people stunted by their spiritual perspective of life. They live in fear, have a fatalistic stoicism, and reflecting a deeply felt belief that life is mostly about survival. In Papua, New Guinea, primitive tribes are animists. They believe a myriad of spirits control life. One lives to appease or avoid the spirits they believe seek to do them harm. Their lives, in contrast to the others I have mentioned, are lived in fear and constant wariness. They never travel more than a handful of miles from their place of birth, partly out of the belief that they might enter another spirit's territory and not know how to act. In an area about the size of Georgia, there are over 750 distinct languages and cultures all bound by the same fears.

I observed a strict burial ceremony in which the body was placed in an elaborately dug hole lined with sticks, leaves and rocks, all to prevent earthworms from making contact with the body. They felt a spirit in the dead person would invade the earthworm, be carried to someone's garden in the body of the worm, enter a food source, then kill the next unlucky victim. Their spiritual perspective of life limits their ability to interact and actually live a life of wholeness.

Given this interconnectedness of the human makeup, it becomes apparent why physical stimulation falls short in providing satisfaction in life. The physical self cannot stand on its own. In relationships, humans are touched at a deeper level. Their whole being is affected. In the context of relationship, physical stimulation enhances satisfaction and fulfillment happening at the deeper levels in the soul. Consequently, fulfillment in life is found in relationships rather than the myriad activities, material possessions, and other stimulants on which our culture has placed its hopes.

If relationships are so important, the question begs to be asked, "What makes relationship, and how do we go about having relationships?" That will be the focus of this book. I want to deal with two aspects of relationship to help define it.

The first is the need to be known. What is being known? Why do we crave to be known? Why are we afraid to be known? How does our culture affect the ability to know and be known? The second aspect of relationship on which I want to reflect is being loved. We will look at what love is, and what love is not. We will look at the cultural substitute for real love and its failure. Finally, we will look at the spiritual sense of love, and how that affects everything else.

We will come to grips with how men and women seek to be known and loved, expose the false thinking behind those efforts, and show how we use and manipulate each other to achieve our goals. We will discover how fully we are already known, reveal an abundant source of love, and find the freedom we need in order to know and love others well.
My desire is to develop a few ideas about relationship in hopes of stimulating thought, self-evaluation, and the opportunity for some to find the source of fulfillment and meaning in life. For others, we may expose faulty relationships and provide impetus to eliminate manipulative lifestyles and shallow friendships. May you be encouraged, and be strengthened in the core of your being. May your relationships be deepened, exciting, and magnetic.

Now, here is a question for you. How do you feel about your

friends and family? Do you find them to be a source of strength or a source of tension, anxiety, or emptiness? Do you know them? Do they really know you?

DAVE COLLINS

THE QUESTION

They walk the halls and shop the malls;

One spirit bubbles like a mountain stream;

One crushed by life like a nightmare dream.

By their face who can know,

does it really show the

question buried deep within bosom walls?

What is their query,

their desperate plea?

Is there one who really cares to know?

Is it safe to reveal;

dare I show from the depths of myself,

the one who is

really me?

DAVE COLLINS

2

THE DUPLICITY OF BEING KNOWN

Webster defines 'know' as "to be aware of; to have information about; to have fixed in the mind; to be acquainted with; to recognize; to have experience; to understand." I might summarize these attributes in simpler terms. It is the state of being exposed. Knowledge is the exposure of the details, the facts, and their interconnectedness giving us a sense of awareness or understanding. In terms of our inner person, this is an understanding we both crave and fear.

Springtime in South Texas is beautiful. The bluebonnets are in bloom creating waves of blue dappled with spots of white. Delicate green replaces the barren browns of winter, sunlight is bright offering soothing warmth, and the air is fresh and mild. Fragrances of fresh cut grass and opening blossoms gently massage the senses. Spring is also a time of trauma for multitudes of high school girls. It is the time when beaches, lakes, and swimming pools are the place to be. It is when they are exposed. It is the first time of the year the new models of the skimpiest clothing is donned. From their perspective, their skin is never whiter, bulges never bulgier, and misshaped parts never uglier. However, they are trapped. They long to be with friends and go to the fun places. They have to wear the best swimsuits. They simply must begin to work on that tan.

A young woman wearing a swimsuit exposes her body. Young men, consequently, have a great deal of knowledge about those girls in a physical sense. If young women did not want to be known, they would not wear bikinis. Many girls, for that reason, never put on a bikini. All the while, these same women exhibit a great deal of fear about their spring and summer exposure. My wife (who does not wear a bikini) still hates to shop for swimwear of any kind. She dreads the thought that a swimsuit by design cannot hide her body parts she deems unattractive. I understand her case is not unusual.

I have observed cameras are often avoided at the beach. Pictures provide public record of everything. The simple act of photography in any situation evokes a common response from high school students. They may clamber to be in the picture, or they may half-heartedly act shy attempting to avoid the picture. When the pictures are displayed, however, everyone shows up, and everyone wants to see himself or herself. Why, if we wish to see ourselves, do we at the same time hide from the opportunity to be seen?

This illustration points out a simple fact about people. They want to be known. They are also afraid of being known. There is a drive underlying our existence pushing us toward exposure. We do not want to simply exist. Mere existence does not make us feel significant or important. When I was young we often said, "I don't want to just be a number." In this country, we all have a social security number, proof of our existence. We want others to be aware of our existence beyond a number. We want them to believe our existence counts for something, that we matter; otherwise, we are left with real doubts, as to our value and purpose in life. However, there are limits we place on what we allow others to know. If they know too much, it may come back to bite us. It is as though we have built fences around ourselves, and few are allowed to enter through their gates. The tension created by the desire to be known, and the fear of being known, leaves us with relationships in flux.

Consider the negative side of being known. It is in exposure that knowledge has its power. It is revealing. Sometimes there are things we feel shame or embarrassment for that we do not want revealed. Neither fear nor joy is provoked in things hidden in darkness, because they are not known. When I go camping, I always take along a flashlight. There are times when I have to get up in the night, and I want to be able to make my way in safety to my destination. I do not want to trip on unseen rocks or miss the bend of a trail. I want to know where I am going. There are times, of course, when this has gotten me in trouble. I have seen little critters in the night which would have gone unseen had I been in the dark. I would have slept in peace had I not been thinking of all those little things I saw in the dark.

Growing up, for me, was a difficult process. I did not receive much praise. There was a constant internal question, large as an elephant but carefully painted white, asking could I really do it. I never thought I could measure up. Fear crouched near my heart ready to pounce with the news I had been discovered, and the whole world would know how hopelessly inferior I was. It happened once in my third grade music class. I had no idea it was ok to lack certain skills such as singing. If my classmates could sing, I should be able to carry the tune right alongside them. I did not know shame was inappropriately assumed for the inability to sing. I sang loudly in this particular class. One day the teacher (Mercifully, I have forgotten her name.) stopped the class in mid-song and said we would do a new drill. Each person would have the opportunity to sing the song solo. We would begin with row number one, right in front, and move down each row, each person standing at their desk to sing their version. I watched and listened as each of my friends had their moment of fame. Little did I know how fast the end to life as I knew it was approaching. My desk was in the middle of the center row exactly in the center of the room.

At last my turn came. I was excited. Here was my chance to shine and experience the joy of song. I sang only a few notes when the teacher held up her hands pointing an accusing index finger right at my nose exclaiming, "You're the one. You sound like a dying pig!" At that moment a part of me died. Standing there in the middle of my little world, I watched all those who knew me cast their vote for my worthiness as part of the human race. For most, it was hard to cast any vote. They were out of control, rolling on the floor with laughter, while I stood in their midst suffocating in my utter worthlessness. At that moment, I vowed never to put myself at risk like that again. I would do all I could to remain hidden, unseen, and unexposed. No one would ever get the chance to know the truth about me....that I couldn't do anything! I spoke very little in school after that day, and only had a few friends.

Telling that story, I can now say sports were a kind of savior for me. I discovered I could actually do one thing very well. I could play football. I could be myself. I could be angry, and actually make emotions into something positive by turning that energy against the opponent. Unfortunately, I had a mountain of desire placed in a molehill of a body, so when my high school career began to wind down, my anxiety began to increase. The one outlet where I had become somebody, and felt value, looked like it would end with the last game of my senior year. I held out hope the quality of my play would be evident to some scout, and I would be offered a scholarship or a chance to play in college. A division one school actually showed some interest in me, but they quickly changed their mind when they came to campus and saw me personally. I could not hide my lack of size. My stature, exposed to all, and was beyond my control. I would have given anything to play, because the game of football defined who I was. Athleticism provided evidence, in my mind, that Dave Collins deserved life.

I did go to college, and never played another down of organized football. Life became a struggle for a time, and I made adjustments. I matured and moved on to newer and bigger things, as one who is working toward maturity should do. However, one day I found out my dad had actually received a letter from a small college indicating they would like me to play for them. There may have even been the opportunity for a scholarship. He never showed me that letter, because he did not think the school would be good for me. He thought he was doing what was best for me. It took years for me to get past his act.

Though I now see how good came out of the experience, I often wish I had never found out, that the light had never revealed how the course of my life changed. Knowing what he had done changed our relationship. It was damaging for us both. I found myself questioning his love, and hiding bitterness for never getting to play football in college. There are circumstances when things are best left unseen and unknown.

We can say something else about knowledge and exposure. The intensity of the exposure affects the breadth of knowledge. Increased exposure produces wider knowledge. A second observation is that greater intensity of exposure gives a greater depth of knowledge. My flashlight with strong batteries will shine farther ahead along the trail than when the batteries are weak. Perhaps a better illustration is the use of x-rays. They expose below the skin and reveal the insides of our bodies. Knowledge provided by penetrating below the skin exposes more to the eyes of physicians charged with the care or repair of our bodies. The deeper knowledge provided by x-rays permits the physician to make more informed decisions regarding the patient's care.

A few years ago, I experienced a surprise event in my life. It was not planned, nor wanted. It just had to be. I had back surgery. Back pain is a fact of life for a member of the Collins family. Almost all my relatives suffer from lower back pain, so it was no surprise that I should stand beside them with the same malady. While walking on a Costa Rican mountain trail in November 2002, I took an awkward step, felt my back stiffen, then pain passing throughout my body. It was nothing unusual at the time. I expected to go through a few days of discomfort as I had for the past 20 years. However, the pain only increased, and eventually walking became unthinkable. I went to the doctor who did an MRI. He said things look compressed on the left side between the third and fourth vertebra. He suggested I see a specialist, who upon seeing the previous test, suggested that I have another MRI with a dye injected into the spinal column. He also made me do a few simple exercises like trying to stand using my left leg only. The conclusion was I had a herniated disc. The diagnosis was reached, through a series of tests made to expose more and more of what was going on in my body. It began with a simple observation. I could not stand up straight. I could not support my weight on the left leg. He looked deeper at the bone structure of the spine, and was able to see abnormalities. He finally looked in a more focused way with the use of dye and x-rays at the soft tissue around the area where those abnormalities had been observed.

The decision to operate was based on the accumulation of knowledge gained by the exposure of intense and penetrating x-rays. It is the intensity with breadth and depth of exposure that gives knowledge power.

In considering the intensity of exposure in the realm of relationships, we find reason for fear. It is legitimate to place some limits to what is seen of ourselves. Some exposure is rightly deemed inappropriate. Public nudity is one example. There is appropriate anxiety, therefore, when we approach those limits. There are also limits placed by personal decisions based on inappropriate reasoning. We may limit what others know about us to avoid their response. It is this inappropriate fear of exposure that harms relationships, and it is to that fear we now turn our attention.

Look at the breadth of exposure. What can we know about people? We can know people at various levels much like varied intensity of light reveals more or less of our surroundings. We can know a person physically. It was physical exposure we examined, in the case of swimwear. We can know what people look like. When we say we know someone, often the image of their face appears in our minds. When we are asked if we know a person, we go through the catalogue of faces in our minds trying to match name with image. Physical knowledge is the primary form of knowledge. It deals with external elements of an individual observed by large numbers of people in a variety of settings. But, we can know more. We can know their personality. We may know what they like, or dislike, and even some of their habits. We can know what they do well, and we may know some of their weaknesses. We can know some of their goals, what they want to do in life, and how they choose to live life. At this level, we can know a lot about a person. However, we all have limits to what we reveal. Here is where we manipulate others by revealing only those things we want known. We try to look good presenting the image we believe will serve us well.

I have a number of relationships with people from all walks of life. My work with high school students exposed me to large numbers of teenagers. The breadth of my knowledge of these students was varied. Some, I have met at functions involving students from all over town. I recognized faces, and with some, I could put a name to the face. With others, I have played sports or watched them in various sporting contests. I had a physical knowledge of these friends. There were some students, in the high school where my work was concentrated, who have been to my home. They have visited with my family, and gone on trips with us. I know one athlete who loved bodybuilding. He also played football, had a little bit of a temper, and did well academically. He exposed some of his soul to me. There are a few students, who have come to my Young Life Club, and have talked openly with me about their belief system. I knew some of their deep longings, hurts, struggles and joys. We have discussed the reality of God, and have known each other at a spiritual level. Yet, with all students, there was a limit to what I knew. Some limits were legitimate. Others were not. Their fear of what I might think of them, if I really knew them completely, caused some to put up barriers. Some kids wanted to be known as my friend. Others did not care to know me at all.

There is some shared knowledge in all relationships. We may know a lot about one another, but only at a shallow level. Such relationships develop only to the point of what can be seen.

There are some, however, that go very deep. The person I have the most exposure with is my wife, Sharon. We are intimately aware of each other. I have seen her deliver our children. I can often tell what she is going to say before the words are out of her mouth. I know the depth of her faith, and the relationship her faith has in her daily life. To picture in your mind what I have just described, think of concentric rings. The outer ring represents the most visible and most easily acquired knowledge. It represents our physical selves that can be touched and felt, like the bark surrounding a tree. The circles closest to the core of our being are much smaller and more difficult to see. Though they are not physically evident, their existence is evident through personality.

Sharon is the person I know the most about, but she is also the one I know most intimately. Ours is a relationship of depth. Depth is the second aspect of exposure on which limits are placed. We can know about the soul of an individual. This involves personality, their likes and dislikes, their motivations, and the various workings of personality creating the character of that individual. This kind of knowledge is acquired by fewer people, because it requires that time be spent with someone in different settings. It requires observation and conversation. The innermost regions of the soul encompass the spiritual aspect of humanity. It is this deepest ring of personality that requires the greatest inquiry and exposure to know. Fewer people are trusted enough to be given access to this side of personality.

I believe there are three levels of depth in relationship. The first is acquaintance. Referring again to students, I have been acquainted with; there were hundreds of kids between the ages of 14-18. I knew some names. I have waved at some in the halls at school and said "hello", because I knew them. I did not spent much time with these people individually, but I spent enough time to develop a shallow relationship. I had few opportunities to see some of these students, perhaps no more than a couple of instances. Some of my daughter's friends have spent a great deal of time at our house. I know when they have been angry with their parents. We have discussed the source of their anger. Others have talked with me about their relationships with girlfriends or boyfriends. In the course of conversation, I have talked about my past, and some of the things that make me who I am. These students have had a more casual relationship with me. A few students have been involved in small groups with me. We have talked about the issues with which we struggle, habits that cause us shame, forces that drive us in life. We have cried at times, and shared very deeply emotionally. We have not hidden much of ourselves from each other. We shared a common faith and perspective on life. These were deep friendships. They are few, and they have required a great deal of time and effort to build. Sharon is my deepest friend at all three levels.

Sharon and I enjoy each other intimately without limitations In the Bible, God describes this most intimate act as "knowing" one's spouse. Adam knew Eve. Abraham knew Sarah. There is no greater way to know anyone in the physical realm. Sharon and I know each other's souls. We have shared the loss of a child through a miscarriage. We have experienced all the emotions, conflicts, and delights associated with raising children, and experiencing life together. We share the dreams of a future together, as well as the mundane events of daily life. Sharon and I know each other at a spiritual level. We pray together. We have pleaded with God together. We have struggled to understand God's direction in our lives. We have shared tremendous joy, and blessings from the God we know.

Our relationship did not just appear at the levels I have described. It has been over 40 years in the making. It began as we became acquainted through mutual friends during our college years. I was attracted to her physical looks, and happy personality. I began to look for her on campus. We spent time between classes playing cards, and laughing with our friends. Eventually, I asked her to go with me to a football game. We dated over the course of our sophomore year learning about each other and discovering we actually loved one another. After graduation, we entered the commitment of marriage enabling us to explore ever-deeper levels of relationship.

There exists an interrelationship between the breadth and depth of knowledge about a person. How does that work? Increased time spent with an individual tends to broaden both the breadth of our knowledge of that person as well as the depth. However, it is possible to know about an individual in all three spheres without going very deep. All of us tend to block the path to the deepest caverns of our soul, for it is in these places where the greatest sense of personal danger exists. It is in these vaults well below our physical surface where our secret thoughts are stored, where nagging doubts about ourselves are hidden, where the greatest longings exist. It is as though a stairwell leading to the depths of personhood exists where each step downward becomes increasingly obscured and more difficult to negotiate. We set up obstacles and protective devices making it difficult for anyone to move too deeply within ourselves. They must prove their trustworthiness each step of the way. Only the most trusted are allowed to see the depths of who we are.

In our high tech world today there is a saying I hear expressing the danger and the lure of knowledge. It says, "knowledge is power." This power drives us away from being known deeply, because that knowledge creates the potential for harm. Potential harm then creates fear causing us to limit what others can know about us. There is a high degree of risk in being known. The risk is in the potential to produce pain, either physical or emotional, as knowledge is used to form value judgments about those with whom we have contact.

The world of sports offers a clear picture of the problem we face in exposing ourselves physically. I became a football coach after graduating from college. Beside coaching the boys on my team, I was required to lead two other coaches each week to observe the next team our varsity would play.

We made note cards of each offensive play they ran, tracking blocking schemes, where they were on the field, and how many yards they needed for a first down. A scouting report was developed serving as the basis for our game plan against that team. Our plan consisted of attacking what we perceived to be their greatest weakness. As we improved in our ability to analyze and "know" our opponents, we improved in our ability to do well against them.

In order to avoid that kind of exposure, making one vulnerable, players in all sports learn to mask weaknesses to protect themselves. I used to love watching Bjorn Borg play tennis. He was stoic, no matter how a match progressed. His opponents could never guess what he was thinking in order to improve their game against him. Boys grow up learning how to appear strong, and confident to mask any weakness they feel is present. Or, they may become boisterous, and in the extreme, bullies. Some boys have joined a sports team even though they do not like the sport. Their aim is to present a strong personal image.

In the world of relationships, physical weaknesses are exploited in the same way. James Dobson in his book **Hide or Seek** discusses the two leading components our society uses to place value on a person. The first is beauty. According to Dobson, nice looking children are treated more warmly than ugly children are. Their worldview is more likely to include warmth and acceptance.

The second is intelligence. Parents assume their child's intelligence and push them to achieve. They must not fail, because failure would diminish their value.

Both beauty and intelligence are physical attributes over which we have little control. We are born with them or without them, yet tremendous energies and money are spent to present a strong image to those around us. Since perceived value for people is derived from beauty, one of the leading industries of our culture is the beauty industry. How many women have spent fortunes and endured countless "unnecessary" operations in the effort to improve their beauty? How many men and women spend hours each week working with a special trainer who promises to make them buff and beautiful? Exercise can become more about looks than about health. Millions of dollars are spent on cosmetics, diet methods, exercise equipment or anything else to improve appearance.

Intelligence, as another cultural mark of value, is often measured by achievement. Parents pressure children to excel in sport at the expense of enjoying a game. They are pushed to achieve. They pay extra to have their child play in an "elite" league, on a top traveling team, under the best coach. An obnoxious parent at a little league game is probably not as interested in the game as he is in his child's perceived value. Some students are pushed to make good grades for what it can get them rather than to help the child grow. A fairly recent development is exposing infants and toddlers to education methods aimed at increasing their intelligence. I have seen articles about exposing children to certain kinds of music while they are in the womb to improve their intelligence.

Knowledge at the physical level is perhaps the easiest to manage. It is the level most people can see. They can know about us. There is a risk of not measuring up, and we may face rejection. However, there are still deeper places to journey in the soul and the spirit of a person. There are more risks in the journey of being known.

DAVE COLLINS

3

DELVING INTO THE DEPTHS OF A SOUL

All of us have an essential need to be known in the deep invisible regions of our being, in our soul. Emotional pain is intensely felt in a soul that feels unknown. We may live with the fear that our souls have no beauty. Of course, we do not put it in those terms. We think along the lines of, "nobody likes me. I can't do anything. Why was I even born?"

In my case, I grew up in a home where excellence was expected of everyone. Perfectionism was ingrained in our way of thinking. My upbringing combined with the death stroke given by my third grade music teacher, was enough to make me truly believe I was worthless, and in all honesty, an unattractive human being. I doubted my abilities and was blind to what gave me value. I also believed every time I spoke out loud, or did anything in front of others, the truth would be painfully evident. I lived in a fearful, hurtful place, as a little boy. So, I developed my own coping strategy. I killed my feelings. It was my way of hiding. I did not allow myself to get in touch with a feeling. I became a very stoic and calm person. Of course, I was able to manage the pain, but this strategy also robbed me of any sense of joy. I went many years through life with a wounded soul unable to experience life. The relationships I had were uncomplicated and simple.

When we have been hurt emotionally, we may hide our pain to avoid giving an adversary the opportunity to repeat the hurt. We may deny the hurt, even to ourselves, in order to prevent anyone from knowing and being able to harm us again. We can live motivated to hide our emotional pain in fear of being exposed to others. Mathematical odds work against us, because knowledge in the hands of many puts one at greater risk than when only one is involved. Observe the hallways between classes in any junior high campus.

Kids in junior high are working hard to find their niche. They are careful what they say, and to whom they speak, for this group of adolescents is ruthless in their socializing. Everyone is very careful to look right and be acceptable. Comments on a physical abnormality such as glasses or braces are brushed off nonchalantly in hopes of avoiding a repeated accusation. Those who fail to do so acquire hated nicknames or repeated jeers in the hallway. Everyone is preoccupied with being accepted, even down to wearing the proper socks. Are they pulled up or down just right? Language is carefully chosen. Likes and dislikes are expressed along the norms established by the majority. Those who wish to be accepted avoid those who fail to meet the recognized standards of the group.

In the business world, men feel they must hide their weaknesses in order to achieve. An honest evaluation of oneself may come across as ineptitude or timidity. So, to climb the ladder, many put on the positive front, never admit doubt or fear, or hide behind an overbearing manner. In our culture, as a whole, men are less inclined to deal openly with emotions or on an emotional level. They tend to avoid exposing their feelings for fear of being labeled weak.

At greatest risk of exposure may be the disclosure of a failed life. Everyone needs to feel a purpose and meaning in life. We all seek purpose in various ways. Our belief system dictates what is important, what we strive for, what we seek in order to make our name and our place in the world. There is the danger someone can know my life to such an extent they may say, "you are a failure." This same kind of knowledge may occur within oneself.

Deep knowledge exposes hypocrisy and shame. It exposes unrealistic life systems, and may reveal a person who lived what may be deemed to be a meaningless life. This is such a grave experience that often men work to avoid even knowing themselves. Over the last decades, much attention has been given to the "mid-life crises." The crises is acted out in inappropriate behavior seeking to gain what has been perceived as lost. Men have been known to squander careers and family in search of something lost from within. Part of the crises is the acknowledgment that a career goal may never be reached, or it may be the goal has been reached and found to be empty. In either case, the crises results from the belief that life must consist of more than previous expectations. The wild behavior is an attempt to find meaning, and avoid facing the issue of personal value. Even financial security or influence cannot satisfy the need to believe our life was significant. Our culture has taken the same course of action. To avoid facing inner weakness, great emphasis has been placed on what is visible in life. We have become preoccupied with beauty, diet aids, and physical fitness. What we do, and what we have, has taken priority over whom we are. Character issues have been deemed less important than personal achievement. Our culture has chosen to ignore its soul both collectively and individually. The exposure may be too painful.

In every case, the inherent risk of being known is its great power in making a value judgment based on the knowledge acquired. Value is placed on each life individually. Others may place the judgment on us or it may be a confirmation by others of our own suspicion that we lack personal value. We may judge our value physically. We may be deemed, beautiful or ugly. We may be judged, weak or strong, susceptible to attack or not. We may be judged, on the soul level to be a good person or not. Our opinions may find favor or be disregarded. Our desires, hopes, and dreams may be considered noble or foolish. Ultimately, our meaning and purpose in the universe is at stake. It is a fearful thing to consider one's value and meaning in life when the results of those value judgments can be so risky. The judgments can lead to rejection, and rejection is a lonely place to be. It may be unfounded and unfair, in which case frustration and bewilderment should be expected. Even worse, the rejection may be grounded on the truth of our pettiness or ugliness. It is a painful thing to see the reality of one's own flawed character. The great fear is to be found lacking regarding meaning and value in the universe. That fear drives us to either hide to avoid exposure or to live outside good boundaries and constraints.

Paradoxically, it is the same power we hide from that we also seek. Knowledge has power to please. It is those we believe truly understand our feelings and know the truth about who we are that we allow to enter the depths of our being. These are the fellow souls who encourage, who lift us up, who offer valued counsel. The same knowledge that exposes weaknesses also has the power to affirm who we are as individuals. The affirming power of knowledge in relationships is in the mutual proclamation of the value of each soul. Existence itself is insufficient in soothing the aching need to know one matters, one has purpose, one has meaning and value, one is significant. Even existence in the midst of opulence and freedom leaves a soul empty, for it lacks the assurance of its value. However small, affirmations of someone who truly knows us provide an abundant sense of peace and serenity within ourselves. Even in the midst of chaotic events in life, affirmation from one who knows us is powerful.

Earlier, I discussed the maze of pathways leading to the depths of our spirits with accompanying tests along the way; tests designed to protect us from potential harm. It takes real work to traverse the often steep and winding way to the depths of a person. It is no easy stroll. We must be committed to the task. We have to understand the difference between feelings and facts. People often talk about the facts of their life giving only a hint at what lies deeper within. If we listen to the facts, and respond only to the facts, we will not get very far on our journey with them. We have to ask questions. We have to talk about feelings, express feelings, and embrace feelings. They are part of the fabric of our selves, and they go to the deepest part of our being. Know someone's feelings, and you will know their soul. We can disarm the defenses, roadblocks on the pathway of the soul by understanding what we feel and who we are while embracing what others feel, and whom they are. Stated another way, we are allowed to know someone more deeply and earn their trust when we reveal honest empathy, and a real understanding of who they are and what they feel. We all want to know others who honestly know and understand us. Their counsel is valued, because it is perceived as valid and helpful. Sometimes, that empathy is gained with hardly a word spoken. At other times, hours of intense listening and sharing produces only slight progress.

I have a friend in Dallas who tells the story of a father and his young son. The boy was at the age where he should begin to mow the yard and gain experience in helping with chores around the house. The time came to operate the power mower for the first time. After giving instructions, the father stood back watching as his son began mowing the front yard making circular swaths around the outer border. In time, he was satisfied his son was competent in operating the mower. The father became distracted by other tasks needing attention. Not long afterward, a telling scream pierced the air immediately throwing the father into action. Knowing something was wrong and anticipating a horrible scene, he ran to his son.

The boy had done well in his first few passes around the yard; however, he eventually noticed the grass clogged in the discharge area of the lawnmower. Reaching down to clear the shoot, the boy put his hands too far in, and the blade, indiscriminate between grass and flesh, cut through the hand.

They rushed to the hospital, but could not save the hand. Worse than the damage to his extremities was the damage done to the boy's psyche. The horror of losing the hand caused the boy to withdraw emotionally. He would not speak and could not communicate with anyone. Some days passed while the boy recovered in the hospital. He showed no sign of improvement, and grew more and more depressed until my friend came to visit with another companion.

The father, on his way out of the room, told the visitors about the accident and relayed his own discouragement about his son's condition. As he talked with my friend, the other man slipped into the room with the boy. It was not long before the two outside began to hear laughter from within the room. They went in to find the boy talking with the stranger, and laughing with him. At that moment, the father noticed the visitor was also missing a hand.

The stranger made an impact, because he knew what the son felt. He made obvious connections and offered optimism and hope to a young boy, because the boy witnessed another who had overcome pain like his own. The healing process began when the boy sensed here was one person who knew how he felt. He had an obvious point of connection having lost a hand like the boy; however, it was the fact that he took time to go to the hospital, sit in the room, share stories, and simply share, his life. We, likewise, find hope and encouragement in those we sense know how we feel.

We humans are not easily convinced of our value. Western culture particularly has robbed people of a reason for being. This culture has invested itself in the search for human origin, and has taken the dominant position believing that man is a product of time plus chance. They say we are here because enough time has passed for a series of accidents to occur. We are all the result of random accidents. Where is our value in that belief system? Life loses significance if it is an accident, then life has no more value than being part of the chain of events leading to a future unknown life form. The result of this kind of thinking is a society where individual responsibility is downplayed, or ignored, where personal happiness is more important than commitment, to another individual. The consequences are an increase in single parent families, a society where freedom to choose is more valuable than freedom to live, where violence and human misery are the mainstays in the entertainment industry. Given this kind of environment, even those who recognize purpose and order in creation and a Creator behind the order, struggle to find personal value and meaning. There seems to be a hunger and a drive to find one's own place in the universe.

Larry Crabb in his book **Basic Principles of Biblical Counseling** states *that man is more than a physical being. He is also a personal being. Man has both physical and personal needs. Included in man's personal needs is the sense of worth. Apart from this sense of worth, men struggle with emptiness, contentment, and a reason to exist.*

We are left to discover our personal reason for existence. There are several options from which to choose. Some feel value is measured by accumulation of wealth and material goods. This view offers some positive appeal. It is easily measurable. Accumulation of wealth provides the benefits of comfort and ease in life. Wealth, however, is left behind at death. It is not connected to the soul of an individual, and cannot be felt. Others take the position that value is based on one's abilities. Those with outstanding abilities, those who are the elite in any category, have value. Though tempting, this position offers little hope, for only a few are the best at anything. We are limited by genetics, leaving the vast majority of people with little value.

Perhaps, it is those who have power, and wield authority, who have the right to claim value. Again, we see certain benefits come with power, but it is a very lonely position. Power isolates. Power is hard to hold. Power is limited to a few, and power is often the result of chance. We may substitute any number of ideas or methods employed to achieve an inner sense of our own worth, but they will all fall short if they depend on what we do rather than acknowledging the intrinsic value of life itself.

Intrinsic value of an individual is validated by the way others react to that individual. When someone chooses to know another, or desires to understand another, they testify to the meaning of that person. Who we are matters. I love to watch people at parties and other informal gatherings. Frequently, small groups form in various parts of the room. Intermittent laughter mingles with peels of belly laughs. Across the room, another group is in the midst of a serious deep discussion. People are telling their stories. The gregarious ones are telling funny stories about themselves or an acquaintance. Others are sharing ideas and thoughts about various issues. They are all telling their stories, expressing their thoughts, demonstrating who they are, and every single story has value.

My wife loves to talk with me. She would rather spend time with me in conversation on a leisurely walk in the cool of evening, than go to the latest movie, go out to eat, or go the hot spot in town. It is in conversation where we share our deepest thoughts and reveal who we are. When I care enough to know her opinions, her fears, or her whims, I am affirming her value as a person. It is not that she has achieved, but simply that she is. She is worth knowing. Her musings and longings have meaning and value, and as I seek to understand her thought processes, I am affirming her life makes a difference to me. One of the hardest lessons I have been learning is that Sharon wants to know my thinking as much as she wants to share her own. When I allow her to see deep within my soul, it is a touching realization for her to know I will allow her in to those deep recesses of my personhood. Interaction at that level signifies trust in who she is. In effect, I exclaim, "you have value and you are valuable to me." It is at those times of deep interaction, when we allow another to truly know us, that we send a silent but deeply felt message. We say I like you. I want you near. You have meaning and impact in my life. I want your input. I want to know you. You are valued by me.

We are left with a choice. We may set up very narrow perimeters around ourselves, never expose ourselves beyond those perimeters, and limit access to our souls. Or, we can take risks, open ourselves up within appropriate limits, face the possibility of being hurt, and find strength from someone who understands who we are. Most of us choose the first option. We play a game with ourselves exchanging the possibility of being known to simply being known about. We accumulate things, seek fame and fortune, or seek control and power trusting those things to fulfill our need to be known. They are all shallow and fail to satisfy.

I recently ran across a description of Paula D'Arcy's

grandmother in **Gift of the Red Bird.** Paula described a childhood filled with memories of her grandmother. Her grandmother was a strong woman who achieved much in a culture with strict limits on a woman's role. She owned and managed a business and lived to the age of 83. She was prim and proper and carried herself with dignity and strength.

In preparing for her grandmother's funeral, Paula was shocked to realize how little she knew about her. Paula's knowledge was limited to things that happened and important events in her grandmother's life. No one knew how her grandmother felt. They could not describe her heart, her desires or fears. The story of who she really was died with her, because she never shared those deep parts of herself with anyone.

What a tragic story! To have lived such a lengthy life, to have left such a paltry understanding of the person behind the clothes and the activities, was a waste and a loss. It is as shallow as reading a list of the dates and accomplishments in the life of Abraham Lincoln and saying we know him. We may read his biography in order to fill in some of the blanks, yet even a biographer is limited in what he knows. We cannot know a person until we also know the "whys" of his life, usually garnered from time and experience together. It is an accurate observation to say I do not sing very often in public, but you know me at my core when you know why that is the case! We must choose to expose ourselves in order to be more than an outline of a life.

A surprising observation is that even the knowledge by others of my failure and weakness can be a source of comfort and peace. Someone who knows us and despite our failures, seeks to understand us makes a clear statement. That friend says our weakness and pettiness do not diminish our value. It is this affirmation that drives us to seek to be known while taking the accompanying risks involved in being known. It is the intimacy of a shared spirit and mutual understanding that can move us to love unconditionally.

Being known actually is a necessary bridge to move from one life to another. A deep chasm separates me from you. We shout across the chasm hoping we hear each other and understand. As long as we have no bridge to cross, there is little connection, and our relationship must remain shallow. The knowledge we have of one another is the road that draws our lives together. I can love you more deeply, the more deeply I know you. Here is why.

1. If I let you know me, I show you that I trust you. It is an invitation to enter my world.

2. If you let me know you, I understand you have opened your life to me, and I may enter. If I guard that trust, I earn the right to enter deeper still.

3. If I know you, I will know your needs, your fears, your hopes. I will know how to love you in a way you can understand. Of course, I also realize with this knowledge, I have a greater responsibility toward you and the ability to hurt you deeply. How we progress in loving one another depends on how I manage this knowledge.

4. Knowing one another and guarding that treasure creates transparency, because I trust you and have earned your trust. We have nothing to fear in each other. We feel secure.

Here, again, is the dilemma. We want to be known, because we want to be more than a number or a statistic. We want to believe life is important, and I am significant in the world around us. However, there may remain doubts as to whether

I matter that much. I can play a game, and reveal enough of myself to ease the doubts. I can manipulate others to know about me, while keeping enough of myself hidden to prevent them from knowing me deeply. By protecting myself from disappointment and rejection, I rob myself of deep satisfying relationships.

Are you really known? Nothing is free. Anything of value comes at a price. Being known involves a risk. Have you seen the risk and, for fear, missed the benefits of being known? Is it worth the price, do you think, to be deeply known? Do you know you are already known completely?

KNOWN & LOVED

When, in disgrace with fortune and men's eyes,

I all alone beweep my outcast state,

And trouble deaf heaven

with my bootless cries,

And look upon myself, and curse my fate,

Wishing me like to one more rich in hope,

Featured like him, like him with friends possessed,

Desiring this man's art, and that man's scope,

With what I most enjoy contented least;

Yet in these thoughts myself almost despising,

Haply I think on thee, - and then my state,

Like to the lark at break of day arising

From sullen earth, sings hymns at

heaven's gate;

For thy sweet love remember'd such wealth brings,

That then I scorn to change my state with kings.

William Shakespeare

DAVE COLLINS

4

LOVE
THE ULTIMATE CHOICE

The weekend was upon me. I was determined to complete my "honey do" list. My children, Kayla and Aaron, had volunteered to help this day. Still very young, they had not learned to avoid work of the garage cleaning variety. Besides, they thought it could be fun to be with Dad. About mid-morning six-year-old, Kayla asked the question I will never forget. A question that, at times, has haunted me. I was sweeping up clouds of dust in my garage when she rather casually wandered up to me and asked innocently, "Daddy, would you still love me if I wasn't your little girl?" I can still see her eyes wide open, questioning. My stomach knots up as I think of my reply.

Didn't Kayla know I loved her? I had told her many times. I had demonstrated my love for her in both visible and intangible ways. Whether or not I loved her was not in question. She was actually questioning the purity of my love. Did it come with strings attached? Must she prove herself worthy of it? Was it an obligatory kind of love? Was it real? Was it honest? The reason the question still haunts me is the answer I gave. It was a quick simple affirmation with little emotion or enthusiasm. Though I answered yes to her question, I wonder if the perceived response was no. She wanted to know, "Do you love me for who I am or do you love me because I carry your genes?" I should have gone wild with excitement, saying I would have picked you to be my daughter out every little girl in the world. In all candor, I must say I have had to learn a lot about how to express real love. I have a deeper understanding of love's meaning and power.

What is love, anyway? Why does it drive men and women, compel them to act, and torment some? Why did Kayla, in her childish simplicity, ask what every one of us is afraid to ask? "Do you love me because you have to, or because you want to? Am I loved simply because of who I am, or do I have to earn it?"

What a frightening question! My observation is people are driven to find love. It is a built in longing in humanity to seek affirmation through the bonds of love. Until we know and feel loved, we will relentlessly seek to fill a ravenous emptiness within. We may not be able to articulate or understand the need or the desire, but we will seek to pack our lives with a multitude of experiences in an attempt to fill the void that can only be filled by love. However, it must be genuine love to satisfy.

Our culture uses the word "love" easily and often. It is rare to see consistency in meaning. Follow as I describe typical cultural expressions of love. Often, emotions are primary, self-interest is the driving force, and compatibility is essential.

Joe and Linda are juniors at their suburban high school. He has been active in sports, and has a positive personality. Linda has been in a couple of his classes, and has been able to talk with him easily. During the fall semester, they began dating, and went to several movies together. Other students in the school know they are both "taken." That spring, enticed by the lure of the season, Joe and Linda find themselves drawn to each other physically. They tell each other of their love and have sex together. They believe love makes it right. Their friends agree. Young people say, "I love you" after only a few dates, believing it is the real thing.

The physical attraction is very real, and very strong. Is this love?

Follow a typical movie story line. Through unusual and unexpected circumstances, boy meets girl. They share an adventure together. Perhaps they share a wonderful time together with friends. Maybe they are drawn to a common cause or common interests. Soon after the recognition of physical attraction, they end up in bed together. Often they separate over a disagreement or as the result of meeting a more attractive person. How easily they move from one relationship to another and call it love! The media presents love in multitudes of shades ranging from I like you to I'm physically attracted to you; you please me; you meet my needs; we share a common cause; I'm committed to you. In most cases, love is characterized by instant intimacy within disposable relationships. It is a feeling based emotion bound up in personal agendas. Commitment and responsibility are disposable in the face of personal sacrifice. Personal happiness has become a chief measure for love. If one is not happy in a relationship, it must not be love. Is happiness in a relationship love?

Like many Americans, I followed one of the most celebrated murder trials of the century. A husband, who had been previously convicted of beating his wife, murdered this same wife. O.J. Simpson actually beat Nicole Brown Simpson numerous times. He felt guilt following those episodes and often went back to her begging forgiveness promising it would not happen again. There are letters he wrote to her expressing his sorrow telling her how much he loved her. I read one such letter in which he admitted there was no excuse for his actions. He told her how much he had enjoyed their relationship lately and how well their marriage had been going. He told Nicole how proud he was of her and how happy he was with her. The night of the incident, he said he had become overcome with feelings stronger than he had ever experienced. He said it was because of those feelings for her that he went crazy.

Uncontrollable passion dominated Mr. Simpson's relationship, with feelings running to the heights. He argued emotions were so powerful within him that rational actions were overruled. Is that love?

This description of love is inadequate. Physical attraction, intense passion, emotions, and feelings, a common cause, or common interests are inadequate explanations for love. They may be a catalyst to draw individuals together, but love moves far beyond each of these driving forces.

Marriage, though still a dominant aspect of our culture, is falling on hard times. Love is assumed to be the glue in marriage; however, the erosion of commitment in marriage in our society has been slow and steady since the 1960's. One half of marriages continue to end in divorce. Attacks on the institution of marriage are subtle and constant. Newspaper columnists suggest posting warning labels on marriage licenses. They have suggested that marriage is hazardous to one's mental and physical health. Comedians poke fun at marriage hinting that couples who stay together are crazy or missing out on life Josh McDowell conducted a survey of young people, and found less than half of church going youth wanted to have a marriage like their parents. Not a very strong recommendation for marriage, I would say. It appears we have a shortage of models truly demonstrating how to love. What does love look like? How can we know it?

The focus, so far, has been on love between men and women. We have not yet mentioned love for our fellow man. How does love properly show itself in friendships?

How do parents really love their children, and how to children love their parents? How is this need satisfied in every day relationships with co-workers, neighbors, and those we pass on the streets?

Since writing these last paragraphs, I have spent months mulling over my own concept of love. Over this time, I have realized how hard love is to define. Most of us think we know love when we see it. Feelings often are the determining factor in attributing its presence in our lives. We attempt to describe it, but a concrete understanding eludes us. I have performed numerous marriage ceremonies, and find the reading of a particular passage from the Bible to be very popular. This passage conveys, for a host of people, the definitive word on love. I am referring to I Corinthians 13, the love passage. This is love, as it is intended to act, love that satisfies. Despite the fact we all fall short of achieving its standards, we are encouraged to strive to follow its example. It provides a picture to which we can compare our own love and a worthy goal to aim at. A careful analysis of its content will be helpful.

If I speak in the tongues of men and angels, but have not love, I am only a resounding gong or a clanging cymbal. If I have the gift of prophesy and can fathom all mysteries and all knowledge, and if I have a faith that can move mountains, but have not love, I am nothing. If I give all I possess to the poor and surrender my body to the flames, but have not love, I gain nothing. Love is patient, love is kind. It does not envy, it does not boast, it is not proud, It is not rude, it is not self-seeking, it is not easily angered, it keeps no record of wrongs. Love does not delight in evil but rejoices with the truth. It always protects, always trusts, always hopes, always perseveres. Love never fails. (I Cor. 13:1-8a)

Beautiful and poetic, these words stir our hearts and

conscience to seek their lofty ideals. It is an action passage, brimming with insights into love, descriptions of love, and things I can do to show love. However, I am still left without love's essence, the underpinning motive providing the power to do these beautiful things for another person. Certainly, love does things, but what is love? I know love is patient, but what is it about love that motivates patience? Love is not simply patience. Otherwise, I could say patience is love, and I know love is much more than patience. The same can be said of kindness. Love is more than any of the attributes listed above, and more than the sum of them. Love is the motivation for each action, the fuel for each, and the driving force behind all of them together. Three different verses from the Bible provide further insight into the meaning of love.

For God so loved the world that he gave his only begotten son, that whoever believes in him shall not perish but have eternal life. (John 3:16)

Love does no wrong to a neighbor; love therefore is the fulfillment of the law. (Romans 13:10)

So, husbands ought also to love their own wives as their own bodies. He who loves his own wife loves himself for no one ever hated his own flesh, but nourishes and cherishes it. (Eph. 5:28,29)

John writes that God's love for the world motivated Him to give something of great value. He gave his son. Love, therefore, places a high value on the one or the thing loved. When value is assigned to a person or object, one places a corresponding commitment to that person or thing. When I was in elementary school, I had an older friend who convinced me reading was fun. A day came when I tagged along with him to a bookstore. Browsing along the rows of books, my eyes were drawn by the bright book jackets of a series of books. They pictured a muscular man surrounded by animals in heavy jungle. I was intrigued and bought the complete Tarzan series by Edgar Rice Boroughs. At that time, they cost $5.00. The $5.00 I spent was close to my life savings. After parting with my hard-earned savings, I proudly carried home my first purchase ever. Not only did I read each book once, I read them again. They started me on a life of reading enjoyment. I still own those books 50 years later, and I am committed to keeping them. They are very valuable to me. Now, as an older person, I recognize the value of my home, and spend what is necessary to insure it adequately. These are all things I say I love, but this love pales in comparison to love for another person. Relationships I value most can be measured by the commitments I am willing to give to them. August 5, 1972, I made vows to reserve myself for one woman. I promised to love and protect her, to care for her regardless of the pain, suffering, wrongdoing, or even success I might experience in the world. Those vows are a measure of the commitments I am still willing to make for my wife. My love for her can be measured by those commitments.

Notice again, from John 3:16, the relationship between God's gift and the world's condition. The gift was given to prevent the world from perishing. The verse does not indicate what the danger is, but it does recognize a choice made by God. If His love were not great enough to offer the gift, the world would be doomed. Love is willing to make a choice on behalf of the one loved. Love chooses for the good of the one loved. It is willing to pay a high cost for the sake of love. Paul points out the aim of love in the Romans passage. Love never seeks to harm. Rather, it seeks the good of the one loved. Paul's point to the Ephesians is love seeks to nourish and care for the loved one to the same extent one nourishes his own body. Paul Brand, a noted physician who has studied leprosy extensively, makes an observation about the body's care for itself. He discovered people who can feel pain act from a "self" oriented perspective. Pain will stop this person from doing anything harmful to his body no matter how badly he wants to do the act. On the other hand, a person who cannot feel pain, yet really wants to do something will continue doing an act that is obviously hurting his body. Healthy people have a built in self-protective stop switch called pain. Our bodies are built to take care of themselves. We naturally choose to protect ourselves, and do what is best for ourselves in the physical realm. Love enjoys the same purpose in the moral realm. True loves seeks the good of others, and will avoid those actions bringing harm or causing pain.

A final observation is love originates from within a person. It is not an external force. I know of no biblical passage indicating love is caused by anyone or anything. It teaches love is part of the character of God. God is love. (I John 4:16) We are commanded to love, thus indicating its presence within our own person. We are called to bring it to the surface. Love is not merely a response to external stimuli such as physical attraction, emotional affection, or nice things done for us. In all cases, love is a choice and is an act of the will of an individual. It does not depend on the response of the one loved or on any other stimuli to be put into action.

Love, we may say, is the motivation from within a person driving him or her to value another to the same extent he values himself. Love will seek to provide all that is good for another, and is willing to make sacrifices from within its own resources for the sake of another.

As we turn our thoughts back to the Corinthian passage, we can explain its message in a new light. It is a description of how love expresses itself.

Love is patient. Patience is the ability to bear a trial. It can endure with calmness even when surrounded by irritants, failures, and unpleasant surprises. It is quiet perseverance. Those who populate the world around us, manage if not maneuver, themselves into becoming irritants. They often fail us. Their failures have impact on our lives, often unpleasant. On the great day of our wedding, my wife Sharon, spent the day in ecstasy as she mused on the perfect man she was about to wed dreaming about wonderful days ahead. Soon after the wedding, something dreadful happened. In her mind, I had changed! In the "up close and personal" world of marriage, my little quirks and faults simply became much more visible. Whereas, before she had not noticed my faults or had been able to avoid them, now she was living with them. I have observed, the closer two individuals become, the smaller the habit, mannerism, or attitude can be before it irritates. Patience puts up with quirks and habits and recognizes their amoral character.

Some habits and character traits are morally wrong and cause real pain. Patience recognizes the flaws in others without minimizing their danger or impact. It works to allow that person to change. It allows time to pass while enduring the results of the poor choices others make. The childrearing process is the consummate practice of patience as we expose weaknesses within our children, provide new modes of operation, and endure their sometimes weak, attempts to improve. Patience does not give up on them.

Expanding our view to the range of acquaintances in our lives, we will inevitably encounter someone with a different temperament than our own. The workplace provides ample opportunity to experience multiple temperaments. One strikes out boldly surging ahead energetically. Another is inquisitive, cautious, and slow to respond to new situations. Patience recognizes the difference and finds ways to accommodate.

In each of these examples, the choice to love enables patience to exist. Its focus is on what is good for the other person and is the driving force to endure. Thus, love allows for individuality and recognizes the dignity in others. It eases the pressure we place on others to perform, accepting their successes and failures. Love, thus, encourages confidence and self- assurance in the person loved.

Love is kind. It is considerate and predisposed to gentleness. Kindness is an expression or manner that uplifts and encourages. It is not always the natural feeling. Kindness, like patience, focuses on the recipient. It is based on the recognition of the inherent dignity in another, a dignity that demands a gentle response or considerate action. My wife's grandmother, in her nineties, had to live in a nursing home. She lost her reasoning abilities, and could no longer care for her basic needs. She did not recognize close relatives any more. In our desire to care for her, we had to move her to different nursing facilities when we moved to a new city. It is amazing to see the difference in care from one place to another. Some see their patients as wards, duties, or part of their job description. In such cases, poor, helpless, individuals lose all sense of dignity and face harsh treatment from staff. In good facilities, the staff recognized the dignity in everyone, even individuals who have lost the ability to function in almost any way. There was a marked sense of kindness and gentleness in the interaction of staff to patients, even when the patients had nothing to offer in response. They honestly loved the residents, and those residents experienced a sense of security and comfort.

Love is not jealous and does not envy. The motive behind

jealousy and envy is selfishness. It is concerned with personal ownership. Envy wants what someone else has. It will not sacrifice for the good of the one they envy. More likely, they will do hurtful things in their effort to gain what the other person has. At times, envy harms relationships indirectly. In the quest to obtain what another person has, envy will ignore a need in a relationship, will give time and effort to the detriment of a relationship, or will become angry with anyone who gets in the way of their quest to obtain. Jealousy's sense of risk or personal loss deprives another's freedom to pursue his or her personal interests. High school relationships often contain elements of jealousy. Girlfriends or boyfriends are closely watched. Conversations with members of the opposite sex are a guarded exercise. In these weak relationships, trust is not present. There is a risk that the friend may find someone else more attractive. An element of self-doubt is present and fear of losing a relationship. The relationship, moreover, is seen more like ownership than relationship. Both members live with insecurity. Personal freedom and growth is restricted. It is a stifling relationship. Love frees another to pursue friendships, and experience a fuller life with others. In a healthy relationship, each person encourages the other to experience a broad range of friendships.

Love does not boast and is not proud or arrogant. Boasting, like jealousy, is a self-centered activity. Praising oneself is a defense mechanism to gain recognition. A proud, arrogant, person is often one whose image of himself is based on self-doubt and insecurity. Therefore, he boasts to build himself up. His arrogance is a tool to put people off and protect himself. The proud person is not motivated to see another person excel, because success in others puts his personal value in question. This competitive insecure perspective pushes the proud person to appear superior to others. Love cannot flourish in such an environment.

We often think of boasting in verbal terms. We picture lofty words or controlling haughty language. Voice inflection and innuendo can be used to put someone on the spot or put them down. However, boasting can be non-verbal activity. How often we see young men and women vying for the attention of just the right person to take to a party, to be a steady, or to be a marriage partner. Such a partner becomes a possession put on display like a trophy in a case. Like a trophy, they are meant to display the presumed power and prestige of the one who possesses them. Just like trophies, they become like impersonal objects collecting dust and soon forgotten.

Love is not rude, uncivil, or unbecoming. Love recognizes the dignity and beauty in others; it therefore, seeks to elevate and encourage. Rude behavior is a means of distancing oneself from another, of discouraging and devaluing others. It often flows out of a haughty spirit.

Love is not self-seeking. It is just the opposite. Love centers on the welfare and concerns of the one loved. It has no hidden agenda, nor requirements, for its continued existence. Love is not manipulative or exploitive.

We are not advocating that love does not care about the actions of others or that the loving person does not desire appreciation, attention, kindness, or needs being met. Love recognizes the desire, but continues in the absence of a particular response. I have noticed when behavior requirements are involved in a relationship certain emotions manifest themselves to a greater extent, particularly the emotion of anger.

If I pay someone to repair my car, there are expectations on my part regarding the work to be done. If I sense the work was done in a sloppy or careless fashion, I will likely feel anger. My expectations are for work to be done in a manner worthy of the payment made. In a similar way, sex can be required in marriage as payment for an expected act rather than as a physical expression of real love. No wonder, for many, the act of sex is such an emotional burden. The act becomes a physical reminder of the emotional hurt and anger brought on by misused expectations. Love freely given, rather than in response to an expected behavior by another, cannot be provoked to anger. It does not keep a record of wrongs, because it is not interested in keeping score or balancing accounts. Love offers freedom and peace to others in place of pressure and anxiety.

Love does not rejoice in evil, but rejoices in the truth. Love's concern for the welfare of another always seeks the truth. Truth is the foundation that produces good. The foundation of truth breeds a sense of faith and security, adding stability in times of uncertainty and difficulty. It provides confidence to take risks. Truth is a bond that cannot be broken.

Because love places such a high value on another, it protects, it trusts; it hopes; it perseveres. Our precious things are placed in secure accommodations. They are insured. They are guarded. Those we hold precious are similarly made to feel secure. There is no greater love demonstrated than when one lays down his life to protect another. Observe a mother who senses danger for her children. Her love will compel her to take whatever risk needed to see to their safety. We place our trust and hope in those things we value. The stock market rises and falls based on the value placed on the economic strength in America. Workers trust it enough to risk their retirement income on investments made in the market. They place their future hope on its trustworthiness. With those we love, we will trust in them and hope in them. Love perseveres. It is not daunted by a cost commitment. It is not halted or diminished by time. It will continue, because it places such high value on the one loved. We marvel at what athletes do with their bodies to achieve a prize. We are astounded by what men and women have endured at the hands of tyrants and evil governments, and still moved on to greatness. Love is no less astounding at what it will endure or do for the sake of another.

5
SNAPSHOTS OF LOVE DONE WELL

We often recognize love, even if we cannot define it. People have seen it and written about it. The following are three independent accounts of people who loved. They are examples of the kind of love expressed in I Cor. 13. Perhaps these beautiful stories will put flesh on words describing love. One account is of a husband who loved his wife. Another recounts the love of a teacher for her student. The final story tells of seven people willing to give their life to love simple tribal people in the remote jungles of Ecuador.

Alex and Anna went out to their back deck to enjoy a cool morning together. Reading the paper together that morning was good, and all seemed well for them. Alex had promised to take the kids to an early movie, so he got up, rounded them up and headed off to the mall. It was not long before he returned and found Anna still in her chair, still reading. Alex joined her again on the deck. Not long after rejoining Anna, Alex noticed two police officers slowly entering his back yard from around the side of the house.

As they approached, one of the officers asked, "Are you Alex?"

Alex said, "Yes."

Anna joined in and said, "Yes, that's him."

The officer then approached Alex saying firmly, "Sir, you will have to come with us now."

They had come to arrest Alex. He was caught completely

off guard, especially hearing his wife say, "Yes, that's him." The officers then explained he was being arrested for battering his wife, Anna, who was calmly observing the whole scenario on the deck.

Then, Alex said, "Please call this number. This is Anna's psychiatrist. She can explain everything."

Fortunately, the officers made the call and soon left the couple to themselves. Alex encouraged Anna to get in his car and then drove her to the hospital where she could receive treatment.

This was not the only occasion Alex had to drive Anna to the hospital. He repeated the process three different times in a long painful series of events that threatened to destroy their marriage. Anna had been diagnosed with bipolar disorder. Her moods, typical of this mental illness, swung to the extremes of manic highs to deep depression. On this occasion, she had been reading in the newspaper about a man who had been abusing his wife. In her mind, the article was talking about her husband, so when he went to the movie theater, she called the police to report her imagined abuse. Alex, thus, never knew what he would come home to or what he would have to face each day while his beloved wife suffered through her mental states.

Alex is not alone in his experience. I have known other men whose wife suffered with bipolar disorder. Some of them simply left. They could not manage the pain and the cost of staying together. My close friend Alex, however, told me divorce was never an option for him. He refused to consider it. His love for Anna compelled him to stay. He confided there were times he was angry, times he wanted to run away, times he felt lost and confused, times he was frustrated, times he wondered if misery would ever end. He said he lived with incessant anxiety, insomnia and despair. His constant struggle was to fill his own tank with enough of God's love to be able to give it away to Anna. Ultimately, it was love that empowered him to survive and be strong.

Anna was not the only one who needed love to survive. Alex shared with me some things he learned about love through their experiences. Life had been lived by him in a vanilla Christian world until the day the door to his world was kicked in. It was the day he was confronted with mental illness. Shame, blame, and awkward moments were sabotaging his most precious relationship. His old ways of handling problems were not successful. They did not work to fix things and make everything smooth again. He could not argue with Anna, try to figure it out, shame her into changing, or do anything to fix her. He could not get angry with the doctors for their failure to medicate her or change her. He could not get them to solve the problem. Alex was forced to learn what would not work to heal their relationship in order to accept what would work.

Alex revealed to me he came to a place where he examined two souls, both his and that of his wife. He could see all the damage and the ugliness, yet he came to this conclusion. Both souls were worth loving anyway. He made a choice. He said he had been too busy "doing" to listen to Anna. Mostly he simply needed to be present for her. He needed to give all of himself to all of her. None of these discoveries came overnight. They were the result of a long process of staying in the battle. They came with great cost and commitment. They came, because he chose to love. Alex told me one of their favorite things to do these days. They walk the streets in their neighborhood that form a figure eight. They walk hand in hand. He mostly "shuts up." He nods his head a lot. He shows up for Anna.

Anna and Alex are still together many years after the police incident. She is still bipolar. But love has made a difference. Anna knows she needs to take her medicine. She knows she needs to take care of herself and listen to her body. She knows she is loved. She also desires to share her love with others. Today she speaks to women about tough issues in a vulnerable way. Alex is aware of how mental issues can kill relationships, so he has become a counselor. He shares himself with others and offers wisdom. Even though he sometimes calls his good friend a putz, Alex loves people well.

Love is important in relationships outside of marriage. It shows up among normal friends who grow up together. Sometimes we see love in unexpected places where position or status exerts pressure to separate. An employer can love his employee, or the employee can love his boss. Students and teachers can truly love one another. There is a famous example of a student and her teacher who loved one another their entire lives.

Helen Keller was born a normal child in 1880, but an illness suffered when she was two left her deaf and blind. Unable to hear or see, Helen lost her ability to understand and communicate with those around her until Anne Sullivan came into her life at age seven. I can picture her life much like my infant children and grandchildren. When they are happy and have everything they want, infants smile and laugh. They are very expressive and brighten a room. Dinnertime however can be a different picture. Infants have no way to say what kind of food they like or desire. They cannot say they are thirsty or want food. They can make gestures and point, but if those in charge do not understand, they have no way to communicate. Frustration is common. Sometimes, food is scattered or probably thrown. Screaming and crying is common for infants. A seven-year-old girl with a similar means of communicating can be disastrous for a household. In 1887, Anne Sullivan walked into the home of a frustrated seven-year-old "infant."

Anne herself had suffered an eye infection leaving her half blind. She came from the Perkins Institute For The Blind and arrived at Helen's home with great understanding about the young girl's frustrations. Unlike Helen's parents who had no personal experience of the pressures and frustrations put on young people by the obstacle of being blind and deaf, Anne understood. She knew the need for love coupled with discipline. Helen had grown up with few rains placed in her life. She was wild and strong willed. Anne would add needed discipline at great cost. She had to deal with Helen's outbursts and wild tantrums. Her patience was tested.

Anne balanced her discipline with love in the only language Helen could grasp. She used touch. There was the obvious touch of the hands as she tirelessly spelled out words with her fingers enfolded in Helen's small hands. Helen had an inquisitive mind and mimicked all the motions, but she had no clue what they meant. Her journey was to discover the gestures had a meaning and every object had gestures to form a word for the object. In the process Anne, often hugged Helen and tried to gently convey love through little kisses and caresses. Those gestures had little meaning for Helen at first. She did not respond and would not sit in Anne's lap for any length of time. It was only after she discovered the meaning of words through her hands that she grasped the meaning of love through a hug. It was a hard battle. In her early journal entries, Anne refers to Helen as a wild little creature and a little savage. She notes Helen's progress as she began to respond to discipline and accept it. Her demeanor became softer. She was quiet for longer periods and enjoyed greater peace as she went through her day. Food, apparently, had been a means of gratification, because along with peace came less desire to eat. Later, Anne's joy and excitement leap from the pages of her journal as she records Helen's discovery that words have meaning. Her love for Helen is obvious as she describes Helen's progress and the warmth developing in their relationship. Anne stayed with Helen as her teacher. After three years, Helen could read and write in braille. She would eventually go to Radcliffe and graduate cum laude in 1904.

Helen in her biography, The Story of My Life, describes her own journey of discovery. She spoke of her emptiness and hunger to understand more of life. She was angry and took it out on those around her. She talked about her inner satisfaction once after throwing a doll Anne had given her to the floor smashing its porcelain head to pieces. She loved the warmth of the sunshine, the smell of flowers and the way things felt. She loved the outdoors. But there was an emptiness in Helen's soul she could not describe; a deep longing that was not satisfied until Anne showed her how to communicate with others. Until she could communicate, Helen was alone in a silent, black world.

Helen describes the day she understood words have meaning. As I write, I can't help but think of the famous move, The Miracle Worker, which came out in 1962. The climax of that movie is what Helen described in her autobiography. After cleaning up the broken pieces of the doll, Anne took Helen out to the water pump to continue her lessons. For some reason the water, rushing through Helen's fingers at the same moment Anne's fingers spelled out water touched something deep in her soul. The movie beautifully depicts the instant transformation of an angry little girl alone with herself to an inquisitive excited discoverer of the incredible world at her fingertips. Helen said she fell to her knees and began pointing at everything trying to feel the letters of the words that now had meaning. These words cannot convey with power like that visual depiction. In the movie, we see a lonely little girl finding life. She simultaneously found meaning in her world and meaning in her life. She forever appreciated her "teacher" for giving such a wonderful gift.

Anne had already loved Helen. She loved Helen when she left home to enter a strange chaotic home in southern Alabama. She loved Helen through discipline. She loved Helen as she met a little girl's need to know and as she taught Helen how to ask and understand. Anne taught Helen how to share her life with others. Helen later learned to love Anne and later lovingly referred to her as "teacher." They remained close until Anne's death. They experienced life together as friends. They shared a mission together working their entire lives to build awareness and ways to help the deaf and blind live meaningful lives. Two lives had been brought together by tragedy, but love created a beautiful story between friends.

Occasionally we run across the story of love so astounding it is hard to believe. We hear stories of men in a foxhole who have thrown themselves on a grenade to save the lives of their friends. We hear stories of incredible sacrifice for the sake of a child or a loved one. Rarely do we hear stories of one dying for a stranger, much less for an enemy. Love at its purest can even lead one to die or risk death for an enemy.

January 8, 1956, five men were speared to death along a remote river in Ecuador by an isolated jungle people known as the Aucas. This tribe had lived for centuries defending its territory from Conquistadores, Jesuits, rubber producers, and the oil industry. Over time, they grew very fierce, protective and isolated. Their culture was built on reciprocation, including a life for a life such that their own existence was threatened by revenge killing among themselves. The Aucas were so violent their language did not include a word for grace or mercy. It was no wonder the white strangers ended up dead. Up to this time, anyone entering their territory risked death. One might wonder why they chose to contact this tribe. Love was the motivating factor.

The five men had come to South America with the desire to help indigenous people know God. They had already been at work with the Quichuas where they had heard about one tribe nobody dared approach. Word was the Aucas, the name given by the Quichuas, (They called themselves Waorani.) were some of the most savage people on earth. Shell Oil employees had been killed and they had killed Waorani. About the time the men arrived in Ecuador, three Waorani women fled for their lives and came to live at the missionary outpost. Thus, the missionaries learned more about this very isolated group no one had tried to reach. Nate Saint, Jim Elliott, Roger Youderian, Ed McCully, and Pete Fleming began to meet and plan how they could contact the Waorani to share God's love for them. Those plans ended Jan. 8 on a beach of the Curaray river where they were all speared to death.

Nate Saint, a pilot, had made contact with the Waorani and had devised a way to exchange gifts from the air. After a number of gift exchanges, the men decided it was time to make physical contact, so they flew to a spot near the Waorani community, landed on a beach, and waited to see if the people would come. Nenkiwi and Gimari went out to meet them accompanied by Mintaka who went as a chaperone, because Nenkiwi and Gimari were not married. The meeting went well. The foreigners even took Nenkiwi on a flight over the village. Thinking it might convey friendship, the missionaries showed a picture of Dayuma, one of the three who had fled the tribe earlier. Mintaka stayed behind as Nenkiwi and Gimari returned to the village.

On the way back Gimari's brother, Nampa, ran into them and questioned why they had left the white men. Nenkiwi was in danger, because he was alone with Gimari.

He therefore responded, "These white men are cannibals. They have eaten Dayuma. They brought a carving of her. It is all that is left of her."

That evening in the village, Nenkiwi created an uproar when he announced his desire to marry Gimari against her mother's wishes. The group had been arguing about what to do with the cannibals and what to do about this marriage proposal when Nenkiwi got angry and began sharpening his spears. He said he would kill anyone who opposed him. Rather than see bloodshed, the men performed the marriage ceremony that night. However, the tension did not diminish. Everyone was in such turmoil about the wedding and the strangers on the beach; the decision was made to go kill the cannibals in the morning.

The five had guns intended for protection; however, when they were attacked by the Waorani men, no shots were fired at the attackers. The men had shared with friends earlier they would not fire, because the natives were not ready for Heaven, and they were. They would not kill Waoranies, even to defend themselves. Nate Saint, Jim Elliott and the others were willing to die rather than kill the people they came to love.

The story did not end with five men dying. It takes an amazing turn Hollywood could not dream up. Gimari who had been at the center of the massacre was the sister of Dayuma. Dayuma had heard about her mother's desire that she return to the tribe and that her life would not be in danger. Dayuma did return and began sharing stories about the white people. She convinced the tribe they would not kill anyone, and that the foreigners would tell them about Jesus and a "new trail" that would be good for their people. They would not have to kill anymore. She was sent back with a delegation of women to invite the two white women she had met in her time at the mission base to come live with their people. Rachel Saint, Nate's sister, and Elizabeth Elliott, Jim's wife, accepted their offer and walked deep into the jungle to complete the work Nate and Jim had begun. With Elizabeth went her young daughter, Valerie. Facing the very real possibility of death, the women said they went to finish telling the people what their men had wanted to say.

Rachel and Elizabeth arrived at their new home with no understanding of the language and no way to take care of themselves. They were at the mercy of a people who had no word for mercy. But, the Waorani wanted peace. They wanted to hear about peace, so they took care of the women and provided food and shelter. Rachel, Elizabeth, and Valerie became part of the tribe, accepted as equals. They could not preach or teach. They had difficulty communicating. They were mostly able to show God's love by their actions. The Waorani knew these women were loved ones of the men they had killed. They were curious as to what motivated these women. How could they forgive? Why would they come in peace? Young Valerie was a great influence as she played with her Waorani friends. She demonstrated the importance of understanding and being understood. Dayuma caught the vision and became a spokesperson. She taught the men not to kill and that spears should only be used to get food. They men understood, and everything changed. They believed God was showing them a new way. The killing stopped. The Waorani turned to peace and began to influence the majority of their tribe to turn to peace. Dawa, the wife of one of the men who killed the five taught, "being speared himself, God's one and only son did not spear back. He let himself be killed so the people killing him would one day live well." Elizabeth and Valerie lived with their new kinsmen for two years. Rachel stayed the rest of her life. Nate's children and grandchildren have also lived in the tribe. One of Nate's grandchildren calls Menkaye, one of the men who killed his biological grandfather....Grandfather. Love today runs deep between the families of those killed and those who killed. It took pure love to achieve so much.

Perhaps these stories have reminded you of someone who loved well. Real love is an incredible gift. It is one of the driving forces in life, hard to find, costly, and treasured when it is found. The ancient Greeks used three different words for love, and each is used in the Bible. Taken together they speak to a whole and complete view of who we are as humans. We are physical. We are also soul and spirit. Eros speaks of romantic physical love. It includes the idea of touch, of the physical attraction between men and women. Phileo contains the idea of brotherly love. It has the idea of friendship and concern for a friend. Souls are bound by phileo love. Agape is the all-encompassing love for all people. It is spiritual. It is the fullness of love I have tried to capture in these stories. In reality, we need all three types. We can substitute one for another or try to depend on one in place of the fullness of love, but we will find ourselves incomplete, lacking, and driven by the need for something more. Our culture teaches that one can find happiness with just the physical excitement of sex; however, ours is a culture that is terribly unhappy and dependent on stimulants and medication to carry on life. We have become mechanical, but machines do not have emotions and emotional needs. We do have emotions and must function as more than a machine.

All babies need to be held. We know the importance of touch, of the security of love expressed through touch.

There is ample documentation of the death of helpless infants placed in sanitary loveless depositories in war torn countries or places in extreme poverty. They were never touched. They were not held and did not hear warm cooing, nonsensical, words from someone who loved them deeply. They died of starvation, not physical, but emotional.

A baby who is held, caressed, and loved for who it is feels something intangible. They cannot possibly put words to it, for they cannot talk. They have not developed abstract thinking, nor can they connect need with action other than to cry when something hurts. Their stomach empties and begins to ache. They cry. Usually the friendly giant comes, holds them, puts something tasty in their mouth, and the pain goes away. They feel another kind of pain. It is not physical. They do not understand it, but it hurts. It is an emotional emptiness causing this pain. They want to be held. They need to know the friendly giant is around, and they are safe.

A baby's need to be fed, cared for, loved, and held is a real thing. All those things provide a sense of security, a sense of peace, a feeling of warmth and comfort. Provided with all these necessities, a baby grows and matures. It puts on weight and learns to coordinate muscle and bone. It learns to associate cause and effect. It learns to think abstractly and interact with the universe. It becomes an adult; however, the adult person's basic needs do not change from those of an infant. We adults still require food, and we still need to feed our emotional and spiritual selves. As if we were still infants, we adults need to be held. Love is what holds us. It is what offers us security, peace, and warmth.

I sit daydreaming at this moment thinking about Elizabeth Elliott, Rachel Saint, Anne Sullivan, and my friend Alex, marveling at the personal sacrifice they freely made for those around them. A sense of peace and quietness must have floated around them like the sweet scent of perfume following the entrance of a lovely lady in a crowded room. Like a small child seeking safety clinging to his mother's legs as a stranger approaches, I see the recipients of these great lovers drawn to the secure strength they possessed. I see loneliness fly away in the presence of these who gave themselves so completely to their friends and loved ones. I wish I had known them all. I want to spend time with them and draw strength from them. I should not be surprised. Isn't that what I should expect? Aren't we always drawn to those rare individuals who have chosen to love? Real love is magnetic. It ties souls together. It affirms personal value and dignity. It encourages greatness and offers freedom in our spirits. It provides a place of comfort in the midst of trials and offers security even when surrounded by chaos. It is unlike the imitation love we experience which demands performance for its dispensation, offers anxiety and insecurity instead of peace, and promotes competition instead of a feeling of completion. As I consider these marvelous lives, I am struck with love's significance. Knowing others may be the magnet that draws us to another, but love is the chord that binds us together.

Perhaps you know someone who loves well. Most of us, however, are not known as great lovers. Even the best of us do not love with complete purity.

Humanity has seen enough to know love is needed and desirable, yet we have not discovered how to do it. We are all clambering to meet our own needs, and in the process, have settled for less than the real thing. Why do we do that?

DAVE COLLINS

6
LOST AND WE DON'T KNOW IT

When I was younger, there was a popular song that lamented the strange state of relationships, "What's forever for", asked a hard question. Why can't people love one another? It talks about people throwing love away as if it were nothing. It questions how we can so easily discard something that is so hard to have. It wonders why something so valuable is not fought for.

Does it seem strange to hear a song like this? If being known to the depths of our being provides meaning and satisfaction in life, and if love is so pleasing and so essential to our well-being, why don't we expend all our energy to preserve and keep it alive? What prevents us from seeing the foolishness of our stubborn pride that drives us to have things our own way at the expense of meaningful relationships? Mankind has studied itself for centuries seeking to figure itself out, trying to piece together the tapestry of what it means to be human. In the effort to understand our makeup, one is left with only two starting points. All our conclusions about the human race will be determined by which of those starting points we choose.

We can believe a conglomeration of atoms, flying randomly through the universe, collided and bonded over eons of time. Some surmise, that given enough time the random development of these atoms has produced man as we see him today. He is the highest known form of life with the most complex mind and social skills in our universe. He is able to reason, to examine alternatives, make decisions, create tools to help him achieve goals, and he is able to control a great deal of his environment, particularly other creatures and plants. In this model, man's intrinsic value is equal to, and no greater than, any other life form in the universe. Meaning is not important. He may be at the top of the food chain able to perform complex tasks, but the only thing giving him value is survival. Continued existence is his chief aim and purpose. In the effort to protect himself, the protection of his environment also claims high priority. Additionally, emotions and mental activity are considered merely chemical reactions influenced by environment and conditioning.

Relationships among humans serve the species no differently than relationships animals or insects have in their world. Propelled by this paradigm, cultures are being studied to understand man's socialization. We observe what relational practices have worked or failed as a means to choose best practices for the present and the future.

The other option, as a starting point for mankind, is that man is not an accident. Rather, he is a product of thought and planning, created for a purpose. If there is a Creator with a design, we must assume value, because all created things have value to their Creator. They were designed and created for a purpose. They have a reason to exist and a corresponding design to achieve their purpose. Mankind's purpose can be understood by either looking at his design, or by the Creator explaining His motives behind His creation.
What is made flows out of the character of the builder. We can look at art and understand the personality of an artist. We assign periods to artist's works by noting the stylistic changes in his work that naturally flow out of his life experience. We study a painting and appreciate the beauty of the work. As we understand the one who put the pigment to the canvas. The work has more impact if one knows the artist, and the message he was trying to convey.

The creation paradigm leads to a different view of man's purpose and meaning. The universe is orderly. It is beautiful. Its Creator must be orderly, and He must appreciate beauty. He created man complete with intellect and emotions, with beauty, and for a purpose.

Belief in a Creator leads to a series of questions. If we acknowledge the existence of a Creator, how are we to determine what the Creator is like? Can He be known? The world is filled with many different religions complete with gods, who presumably have created this planet and all who walk upon it. Is it true, as many would contend that it was all done by God? This God has been given many names by various cultures, but His name is irrelevant?

If God is real, we must assume He has characteristics defining who He is and who He is not. You and I can make the same claim about ourselves. There are physical characteristics making every person in the world unique and knowable. Courts have long used physical characteristics to decide the guilt or innocence of an accused. In earlier days, judges depended on eyewitnesses who witnessed a crime, and could recognize physical features of the perpetrators. Later, fingerprints were discovered. Our skin, like snowflakes, develops in unique and different patterns in every individual. However, even fingerprints; do not tell the whole story. Today, we have discovered how to map DNA, found in every cell of every human. It is unique in every person, and acts as a blueprint for the physical body of every human. Everyone human contains a unique map shared by no one else. DNA is in each cell of every individual. It never changes within an individual. It is never duplicated, except in the case of identical twins. That is why they are identical.

Not only do we have a personal physical blueprint, we have

an emotional self as well. We all possess a unique personality, and though twins are identical physically, even they possess unique personalities. Everyone, including identical twins, make choices according to their personality and react individually to their environment. We are all different emotionally. I think differently than you. I have my own values, likes and dislikes. I am attracted by stimuli in ways that do not faze you. I have my own fears, my own set of aspirations, and things I believe will make my life significant. Though we may share cultural similarities, our personality is not bound by culture.

Understanding we all have physically visible and spiritually invisible sides to our self. we can describe a person at multiple levels. Therefore, you and I can both determine if a person truly knows us or not. Suppose someone approached you stating he knew me.

You might say, "Well, can you describe Dave to me?"

They might say, "Oh, Dave is about six feet tall. He weighs 170 lbs. and has red hair. He is the most outgoing kind of guy, and the life of the party. He loves to be the center of attention, always seems to be around a crowd of people, and attends all kinds of cultural functions."

I would tell you, "I'm sorry, that person doesn't know me at all. I don't look like that. I definitely would not be described as the life of the party since I am actually more the introverted type. Though I do love people, I do not really enjoy being in the spotlight, and would much prefer to serve and be in the background."

I am knowable as the person, Dave Collins. God, if He exists, is knowable for who He is. God has revealed Himself; He has called Himself by name. Though lacking a physical body, He is spiritual. He has personality and has defining character traits. If God is a person with personality, He is describable and knowable. We cannot accept the idea that sincere belief in God, whatever His name might be, is valid. We cannot accept the idea that all concepts of God have equal value, that all gods mare the same but have different names, when the various "gods" have differing descriptions of themselves and various desires and goals for man. We would have a God suffering from multiple personality disorder, and our beliefs about God would become no more than a guess. He would be unknowable. Furthermore, if we cannot know God, it becomes impossible to know man's purpose and meaning, assuming we believe creation flows out of who the Creator God is.

Our starting point is crucial. We must grapple with two questions. Is it possible to sift through all the data, all the beliefs, all the claims, and know a true God and Creator of everything? Or, are we created at all? Are we, as the theory of evolution states, in the process of moving along a chain reaction governed by chance and yet to be completed?

I believe there is a definitive answer. We can know, because the true God has revealed Himself, physically, and in writing to mankind. He has provided us with enough information to know who He is, and who we are. He actually wants to be known. He has provided the answer to the question of why we humans have such a difficult time knowing and loving one another. God says He created man. What's more, God says man is the crowning glory of all creation, because God made man in His image. Man, therefore, reflects the character and personality of the creator God. God says He is love. He is a relational, personal being who wants to know us and love us. He wants us to know Him and love Him in return. God explained how creation was intended to function. Mankind was given the ability to make choices.

The problems men face, including our relational issues, can be explained by understanding the choices man has made. We have chosen to reject God, and in our minds recreated Him to our own liking. We have refused to know God as He is, or love God for who He is. Consequently, we have lost a sense of whom we are and how we are to love. The story is written in the book of Genesis.

It says. *"So God created man in His own image, in the image of God He created him; male and female He created them." (Gen 1:27)*

Man is not an accident or chance development. He is significant. In all creation, man alone bears the mark of God, the unique mark of "image." People say my son, Aaron, is the "spitting image" of me. Mostly, they are referring to physical appearance. His facial features are very similar. His body has some similarity, but we are very different in many ways. He is much larger than I was at his age. People comment frequently about our similar mannerisms. We have the same gate as we walk. We carry ourselves similarly, and have the same gestures, especially how we use our hands. Our interests run along similar paths particularly in our competitiveness. We both love football and other sports. Aaron's outlook on life has been shaped by my views. As he has progressed from adolescence to adulthood, his views, though influenced by me, have been processed and internalized to be his own. At this point, he still has much of my perspective on life. This is all to say that "image" is much more than a physical thing. The image mankind bears to God has nothing to do with physical characteristics, because we know God is a spirit. He has no body. Our "image" is what separates us from the rest of life. We are creative. We have logic and the ability to think abstractly. We can make choices based on a moral sense. Every man alive believes some things are right, and some are wrong. Morality has not evolved. It is part of the image of God. It is a reflection of the character of God, because everything good flows out of the goodness of God. God, therefore, defines what is good. Our conscience and our struggle with guilt is real and true, because it is based on the truth of our image. When we do wrong, we violate who we are and whom we reflect. Guilt is the result. God says more about man in Genesis.

God said, "It is not good for the man to be alone. I will make a helper suitable for him." Now the Lord God had formed out of the ground all the beasts of the field and all the birds of the air. He brought them to the man to see what he would name them; and whatever the man called each living creature that was its name. So, the man gave names to all the livestock, the birds of the air and all the beasts of the field. But, for Adam no suitable helper was found. So, the Lord God caused the man to fall into a deep sleep; and while he was sleeping, he took one of the man's ribs and closed up the place with flesh. Then, the Lord God made a woman from the rib he had taken out of the man, and he brought her to the man.

The man said, "This is now bone of my bones and flesh of my flesh; she shall be called woman, for she was taken out of man." For this reason, a man will leave his father and mother and be united to his wife, and they will become one flesh. The man and his wife were both naked, and they felt no shame." (Gen 2:18-25)

Man is built for relationship, because God is relational, and man reflects that aspect of the image of God. To help man understand the importance of relationship, he asked Adam to name all the animals. In the process of naming the animals, Adam saw the beauty of nature, and the created world around him, and he discovered something was missing. Was

God sending Adam on a frantic search for a suitable match as if something had been forgotten? No. This appears to be an object lesson for Adam. I picture him observing all the animals with a growing sense of loneliness. Pets are delightful, but they cannot meet our deepest needs. Adam experienced a clear lesson understanding his need for relationship with someone like himself, a suitable helpmate.
When God woke him from sleep to present Eve, I do not imagine Adam looking her over saying, "Well, yes God, this looks like what we have been looking for. I think she will do just fine." I see a man going "WOW!!! She's perfect! This is what I have been looking for all along! Thanks God. You're the greatest!"

I think he was profoundly aware of his need for relationship as he named animals internally comparing each one to himself. He recognized she was flesh of his flesh. They were alike. They would find companionship and experience life in a more meaningful way united to one another. Nothing was hidden between Adam and Eve; they were naked. This is obviously referring to physical appearance, but I believe they were completely uncovered emotionally as well. They had nothing to hide, and knew each other completely. They had no shame and nothing to feel shame for, because their life was being lived as God intended.

God told Adam and Eve they had free reign of the garden with one exception. One tree in the center of the garden was off limits. They were not to eat its fruit. God had given them everything they needed. They could go where they chose and do what they wanted. He was there with them, and often walked with them. They had each other. They had God. They had purpose and dignity in their work as God's gardeners. They knew each other completely, and loved each other fully. But, things changed.

Now the serpent was craftier than any of the wild animals the Lord God had made. He said to the woman, "Did God really say, "You must not eat from any tree in the garden?"

The woman said to the serpent, "We may eat fruit from the trees in the garden, but God did say, "You must not eat fruit from the tree that is in the middle of the garden, and you must not touch it, or you will die."

"You will not surely die," the serpent said to the woman. "For God knows that when you eat of it your eyes will be opened, and you will be like God, knowing good and evil." When the woman saw that the fruit of the tree was good for food, pleasing to the eye, desirable for gaining wisdom, she took some and ate it. She also gave some to her husband, and he ate it. Then the eyes of both of them were opened, and they realized they were naked. So, they sewed fig leaves together and made coverings for themselves. Then the man and his wife heard the sound of the Lord God as He was walking in the garden in the cool of the day, and they hid from the Lord God among the trees of the garden. The Lord God called to the man, "Where are you?"

He answered, "I heard you in the garden, and I was afraid because I was naked, so I hid."

And He said, "Who told you that you were naked? Have you eaten from the tree I commanded you not to eat from?"

The man said, "The woman you put here with me- she gave me some fruit from the tree, and I ate it."

The Lord said to the woman, "What is this that you have done?"

The woman said, "The serpent deceived me, and I ate."
(Gen 3:1-13)

The scriptural account gives the basic facts of what happened. According to this account, Eve knew God's command not to eat a specific fruit; however, Eve added to what God had actually said. I can imagine what may have gone through her mind. I can see her building a case against the fruit. "I can't eat it. That is dangerous stuff. I better not even touch it. Did God say, don't touch it?"

In the end, she was faced with a dilemma. God had said not to eat the fruit. The serpent had said not only was she permitted to touch it, but that she should eat, the fruit and it would be a good thing to do. Eve had to choose, "Do I believe God, or the serpent?"

They had said opposite things. What should she do? I picture Eve wrestling with the problem something like this. Perhaps she wandered over to the tree. She examined it. The tree looked good. It did not look dangerous. Building her courage, she carefully and slowly reached out, touched it, then quickly retracted her quivering finger? She didn't die; nothing happened. Maybe the serpent was right. It would be nice to have wisdom and be like God. How nice to know as much as Him. She made a choice. In her mind, the serpent was right. God was wrong. She ate.

Adam made a choice as well. The scriptural account indicates he was beside Eve when she ate. Did he try to talk her out of eating the fruit? If he did, he lost the debate. What was his reaction as he watched her take a bite? God told him the results of eating would be death. We do not know if God explained death to Adam and Eve, and they. had never experienced death to know what it was. Maybe Adam watched Eve, to see what death looked like. Did he sit back and watch? Nothing seemed to be happening to Eve. She appeared unchanged. He may have lost confidence in God, at that point, and ate. He may have had a full understanding of death. Perhaps he watched Eve, the answer to his former loneliness; eat the fruit knowing God would take her from him. He may have thought through the difference between life with Eve away from God verses life with God apart from Eve. Whether Adam understood death or not, he chose to live life with Eve apart from God.

The results were immediate. They saw nakedness in a different light. They knew shame, for having chosen life apart from God; they no longer reflected the pure image of God. Not only did their relationship change with God, but between each other as well. They experienced valid guilt. They saw themselves as imperfect, and wanted to hide. What had been beautiful before became a source of shame and guilt. They covered their physical bodies. They began to cover themselves emotionally.

Picture God, strolling leisurely through the garden, humming a happy tune. Adam and Eve hear him coming, and hide in the trees. Suddenly Adam hears something he has never heard before.

God asks, "Where are you?"

God always knew where His children were. He knew this day as well. I imagine Adam and Eve's relationship with God before they ate the fruit. My mental image is children running up to the Creator giggling and jumping into his arms, just as my children used to do when I came home from work. Clambering to be near Him and enjoy His company was normal, and the usual experience in the beginning. They did not run to him this day. They ran to hide. They could not face him. Where once there had been joy, there now loomed fear.

"Where are you?" Asked God.

The question was for Adam's sake, not His own. The question was more than about physical location. His emotional and spiritual location had to come to mind. The question forced Adam to see the consequences of his disobedience. He had indeed forfeited his relationship with God for Eve. Adam had to answer the question. Adam knew he was hiding from the Creator he had always run toward before. At that point, Adam admitted his guilt and nakedness before God, but did not take full responsibility.

"The woman you brought to me that day when I slept, she gave this fruit for me to eat. God, you have to take some of the guilt for this situation. This woman is your fault. You made her. You brought her to me. She did it. She is at fault more than me."

Bitterness had sprung up between Adam and the most precious One he knew. Toward the woman he once exclaimed was flesh of his flesh, he now shoved all the responsibility for the choice both had made. The Bible has nothing to say on the issue, but I have often wondered what it was like between Adam and Eve that night as they went to bed together. I wonder how Eve felt about Adam blaming her for everything. What walls began to develop, between them that day? When Adam blamed God for creating an imperfect woman who was to blame for this event, he wounded the wonderful relationship he had previously with Eve.

Eve's response to God was no better. She too tried to shift her guilt.

"It was the serpent. He tricked me," she said. Though she never blamed Adam or God, she refused to take responsibility for her own choice. She had already chosen the serpent over God.

Many scoff at the Bible's explanation for man's beginnings, and its account of man's plight. They say this was ancient man's attempt to explain what he could not understand. It is too simplistic. Modern man thinks he has a more scientific and clearer answer for who we are. Truly, this is a simple explanation. Yet, I have found no better answer to man's relational struggles. Furthermore, today's arrogant claims based on science and knowledge have not done anything to clearly explain or improve man's condition in the world.

Thousands of years after this was written, a new passage was added in the New Testament. It amplifies the significance of the broken relationship between God and man. In the book of Romans, we read....

The wrath of God is being revealed from Heaven against all the godlessness and wickedness of men who suppress the truth by their wickedness, since what may be known about God is plain to them, because God has made it plain to them. For since the creation of the world God's invisible qualities His eternal power and divine nature - have been clearly seen, being understood from what has been made, so that men are without excuse. For although they knew God, they neither glorified Him as God nor gave thanks to Him, but their thinking became futile and their foolish hearts were darkened. Although they claimed to be wise, they became fools and exchanged the glory of the immortal God for images made to look like mortal man and birds and animals and reptiles. (Rom. 1:18-23).

Man lost his close relationship with God. Though man's

conscience convicted him morally, he refused to admit that what he knew to be right or wrong actually flowed from the character of his Creator. Though men looked at nature and saw the fingerprints of their Creator, they refused to know Him as He really is. Men only imagined what God is like. They made totem poles to worship animals, and began to worship the creation rather than the Creator. This way of thinking is not limited to primitive tribes. In our modern world, we men follow the same line of thinking to the ultimate limit. The Humanist Manifesto, written in 1933and restated in 1973, claims God is nothing more than man himself. Men and women through the ages have not known God. Refusing to know God, we have refused to give Him glory, and we have lost our own sense of being and purpose in the process.

If God really did create, and if He really is that powerful, doesn't He already have glory? How then, can man give God glory? It is given by acknowledging the truth that is evident about God. We reflect back the truth. We worship the true God. Refusing to know God, we also refuse to love Him. Men refuse to give Him thanks. This refusal is an indication of our heart's desire to be rid of God. We do not want to owe Him anything or acknowledge our need for Him in any way. In our pride, saying thank you to God is too humbling. Continuing in the Romans passage, we read...

Therefore, God gave them over in the sinful desires of their hearts to sexual impurity for the degrading of their bodies with one another. They exchanged the truth of God for a lie, worshiped, and served created things rather than the Creator - who is forever praised. Amen. Because of this, God gave them over to shameful lust. Even their women exchanged natural relations for unnatural ones. In the same way, the men also abandoned natural relations with women and were inflamed with lust for one another. Men committed indecent acts with other men, and received in themselves the due penalty for their perversion. (vs. 24-27)

Having exchanged the truth about God for a lie, mankind began to worship things rather than God. We now seek happiness in clothing, homes, jewelry, etc. We worship things, seeking fulfillment in them rather than giving thanks to the One who gave us our senses that allow us to enjoy His creation. Having lost sight of God, man has lost sight of himself. He has become foolish. Sex has lost its beauty today. It is not seen as a glorious union between two people, but rather as an end in itself. Pornography has grown to be one of the most lucrative businesses in the world. Children are experiencing sexual relations at younger ages. Marriage is not considered important. Mankind has lost sight of what it means to be male and female. We do not recognize the wonders of our differences and confuse the dignity of gender. The feminist movement has sought equality with men leading to the denial of their own uniqueness. Marriage, which should celebrate gender differences, is being proclaimed as nothing more than a contract between two individuals regardless of gender. Men do not know how to be men, and women do not know how to be women.

Romans goes on to say...

Furthermore, since they did not think it worthwhile to retain the knowledge of God, he gave them over to a depraved mind to do what ought not to be done. They have become filled with every kind of wickedness, evil, greed and depravity. They are full of envy, murder, strife, deceit and malice. They are gossips, slanderers, God-haters, insolent, arrogant and boastful; they invent ways of doing evil; they disobey their parents; they are senseless, faithless, heartless, ruthless. Although they know God's righteous decree that those who do such things deserve death, they not only continue to do these very things but also approve of those who practice them. (vs. 28-32)

Refusing to know God has led man to lose his sense of place in the universe. We do not know how to live and make choices in harmony with others. This list of man's evil practices indicates a mindset of placing himself in the center of the universe. Everything revolves around "me." Enmity and strife are the natural consequences, and relationships suffer.

I do not know anyone who claims this passage as a favorite. I know many who try to throw it out, ignore it, or change its meaning. It is a hard pill to swallow. Mankind has lost its ability to love one another as God intended, and has turned to evil and hurtful relationships. There are some who claim this passage is ancient history, that it takes a very narrow view of humanity based on an old religious bias. In our generation, we deny its truth and call it narrow minded or mean spirited.

Secular Humanism is alive and well today. Their original Humanist Manifesto, written in 1933, made several claims. It holds the view that the universe evolved over time by chance. It rejected the idea that man is anything beyond physical, and claimed religious ideas were the result of cultures and their influence. They asserted science is man's only way to know the reason for existence or how man can best manage life. In 1973, humanists further added that religion may have good ethical traditions, but generally hinders man from being all he can be if allowed to think freely. They categorically denied the existence of God and asserted that man alone can save himself

Since the writing of these documents, the world has seen genocide in Europe, Africa, and in Asia. Terrorism is becoming a fact of life all over the globe. Violence against innocent victims is perpetrated as a means of gaining political goals. Though knowledge has grown exponentially, life expectancy has not progressed significantly beyond what it was at the beginning of this century. Aids has killed millions in Africa and Asia, and continues to grow despite the best efforts of medicine. Despair is rising in western societies, and the use of drugs, both legal and illegal, to alter or control emotions dominates our world today. In fact, the post-modern age is characterized by despair and a pragmatic search for personal pleasure and comfort. Life's value formerly considered intrinsic, has been replaced with the phrase "quality of life." That same phrase is used as justification to put people to death. There is increased gender confusion, homosexuality issues, and the deterioration of stable family units. Whether one signs the Humanist Manifesto, or simply adopts its tenants, he must accept the consequences of those beliefs. Man still refuses to acknowledge that God is God. In this manifesto, the writers have removed all possibility that a God might reveal Himself in something other than a scientific manner. For humanists the possibility that God came personally to tell the world about Himself is beyond reasonable thinking. In refusing to know God as He is, man has not improved but followed the exact sequence of consequences God revealed would happen.

We humans do not want to admit our woeful condition. We do not want to admit our condition is the result of exchanging the truth of God for a lie, and refusing to consider it worthwhile to hold on to the knowledge of God. The number one problem in all human relationships is that man has lost his relationship with God. Out of that broken relationship flow all our difficulties with our fellow men and women, and with ourselves.

The difficulties begin with me. Having lost sight of my Creator, in whose image I am made, I have lost sight of who I really am. Individually, we have a crisis of value, purpose, and identity. If we are no more than an evolved slug, what reason do we have personally to excel? What reason do we have to live? What reason is there for personal sacrifice or benevolence? Personal comfort and pleasure become our goals. It may sound noble to say we excel for the sake of mankind, but people I know are not very concerned for humans several generations down the line. We live for today, or for the years we recognize as our own. Apart from a Creator, nothing provides intrinsic value to individuals. There is nothing beyond consequences imposed by one's family and culture for doing wrong compelling man to not do evil. We have even less compelling us to choose high ideals, moral virtue, and self-control. The fear of being caught, of being punished, or of being rejected for our actions combine to apply certain pressures to live nobly. However, those same cultural forces cause racial wars, genocide, and all kinds of evil. Apart from the existence of a moral Creator, what reason is there to oppose evil in one's culture?

Consequently, individuals seek from within themselves something to give the value they crave. It is a daunting task. Where should the search begin? Suppose I have a great talent for catching fish. Fish catching might give me some value. Suppose my family moves to the dessert where my talent cannot be put to use. Have I lost value as a person? What a feeble person I become if geography determines who I am, and my reason to exist. Some men are born with athletic skills. Bo Jackson, a wonderful athlete I loved to watch, was known for his strength, speed, and natural hand-eye coordination. He could run faster than most men. He could lift more weight than other athletes lift, and do incredible athletic feats without working out as hard as others work. He was a natural. Television commercials told the story. Bo knows. Bo can do anything. I watched him break away in a football game on an amazing run. The last defender for the opposing team was able to tackle him, just like he had been tackled hundreds of times before. At the end of the play, Bo did not get up as usual. His hip bothered him. The hip socket had been damaged in a rare injury. Bo would never play football again. He had to have the hip replaced, and his athletic days ended prematurely. Did Bo Jackson lose value as a man when his athletic skills were cut off by an accident? What a fragile sense of being we would have, if injury were all it took to rob us of meaning in life.

Is physical beauty the thing that gives us value? Models and movie stars make millions of dollars based on their looks, but what happens when they age and beauty runs its course? How are they to see themselves as a person? What a tenuous frightening position to be in if value and purpose for life is so easily lost. We have a self-image crisis, because this is exactly how our culture places value on humanity.

Very few people reach the pinnacles of achievement. How many can honestly say ....I am one of the best? Everyone who lives in such a system is subject to the whims of society, because changing cultures set standards for what is valuable and admirable. Fashion trends come and go. Men and women enslave themselves to the current fashion gurus in order to be acceptable and find affirmation for who they are. Individuals become slaves to the opinions and desires of others, and risk never knowing whom they are inside. They obsess with what they think is good and right, rather than seeking what is right based on who God is. Many have lost sight of who they are as a person, as though they were actors constantly changing roles in a play lasting some 70 years.

In the end, without God, we must depend upon the

affirmation of society to declare we have value, we are lovely, we have meaning in life, we are worthy of relationship.

Assuming men lack intrinsic dignity and personal identity, we face the task of assigning meaning and dignity to those with whom we associate. Why should I value another person? Why should I treat them with respect? Why should we agree that race wars are good or bad? After all, identifying the strongest race would help ensure the survival of humanity. Failing to recognize individual intrinsic value forces everyone to identify something special in another person in order to value that person. We tend to look for things we like about a person. Most often, we choose externals because external visible qualities are easy to identify and quantify. They are how people look, how they dress, how they talk. Externals are what people can do, what they can achieve. It is more difficult to know the deep character issues, the inner qualities and simply accept their human intrinsic value. This kind of judgment can go array. When I consider the character of some of our sports or entertainment "heroes" today, I cringe. It can be a difficult road for some. The number of wonderful young men and women in high school who have a relatively limited social experience in dating relationships amazes me. As I get to know these people, I often find them they are often witty, fun, caring, people I would assume most would like to know. They happen to be rather ordinary looking physically, so the. external value placed on them limits their relationships. Minorities face a negative bias daily in life. I heard of an executive, a black man, who would occasionally shop after work. He dressed in suit and tie, carried a briefcase, and walked through stores without incident. If he went shopping on Saturdays dressed in shorts and casual attire, he would often be followed by security personnel, and be treated like a suspected shoplifter. Another executive shared with me about a time he was confronted by a minority employee about his prejudice. She said he never greeted her with the same cheery hello he gave the other employees in the building.

Because we have lost touch, with whom God is and what He is like, we have lost the underpinning values on which to build relationships. We are still relational. The need does not go away, but our ability to grow authentic relationships is weakened. We compromise our true design for what we think will work.

DAVE COLLINS

7

THE WEAKENING OF RELATIONSHIPS

When we fail to acknowledge people have intrinsic value, relationships are risky and shallow. We are led to look for things we like about people, rather than ways to love people. We tend to know "about" a person rather than know the person. Relationships take on the characteristic of a chain. It is only as strong as the weakest link. We quickly abandon someone who is a weak link, and move on to another relationship. There is no real advantage to befriending someone who cannot give something to us. Consequently, we tend to look for what "I" get out of the relationship. People come and go in our lives with too much ease.

Relationships become risky if they are based on a fragile foundation rather than the foundation laid out by our Designer. I become vulnerable if I reach out to someone who does not respond as I wish. If I sacrifice myself, there is no guarantee they will respond. They may never choose to meet my need. Relationships are at risk when based on what a culture declares as worthy. What if they say I do not measure up? What if I do not know their measuring system? What if their system requires something my personality cannot deliver? How can we know what another person likes in people? What must I look like for that person to respond to me? One lives with constant pressure and tension trying to fit in. Relationships become tenuous and fearful. We may not be allowed to change. Things beyond our control, aging bodies can kill a relationship built on looks. There is the fear that, "If you really knew me, you would not love me." There is fear of discovery. One day I may give myself away, and lose the relationship. The difficulty with living within these tensions is the strain they place on relationships. Additionally, my self-esteem is at risk if my value and dignity depend on the affirmation of others.

We have developed relational games to help maneuver through this tough existence. We have four possible ways to manage personal relationships.

The first is that we allow others to know and love us as we work to know and love them. This first paradigm is lost if we refuse to know God and live according to His design. Most live with the remaining three. We can put ourselves in a position of being loved but not known. We can be known, but not loved. Some are neither known nor loved. Even as we identify these options, we must recognize that apart from knowing God, to be known and loved will more likely look like being known about and being liked.

Loved but not Known

This kind of relationship is better described as one who is liked but not known, is illustrated by the following story. I knew a young man who played football in high school. He was very talented and had all the skills needed to excel in the sport. Mike became well known on campus and thrived in the limelight. Popularity followed his press clippings, and propelled Mike to a fast life. He was invited to every party, and began drinking heavily. However, sometime after his junior year, Mike began to realize his lifestyle was not good for him, nor did he enjoy it. Life never changed for him in high school, because he felt trapped. He liked the notoriety and the popularity. He was afraid people would not like him if he changed the lifestyle or refused to go to some of the parties. Mike was frustrated realizing he could not be who he truly wanted to be. He was known as a "jock" who partied, and that was it. He did not know how to express himself, or be someone other than what the crowd had wanted from him. He did not break out of the mold until he went to college, and started a new life with people who had not known him before. He still played football well enough to excel on the national level, but his lifestyle changed dramatically from what it had been in high school. He developed intellectual interests, and took part in creative pursuits outside of sports. He broadened his experience and expressed himself in various pursuits.

It is easy to become trapped like Mike was in high school. The easy thing to do is find ways to be liked. If we have a talent, there will be others who appreciate that talent enough to socialize with us. We can develop social preferences that throw us into a like-minded crowd. Going to plays or the opera, attending sporting events, or volunteering in service organizations draw folks with similar interests together. Once we find ourselves in a particular mix of people, the tendency is to conform to that group's expectations. If we find ourselves differing with what is defined by the group as the norm, it is very risky to voice our differences. It is easier to go along with the crowd than risk being known. There are times when one is tempted to remain silent until the prevailing acceptable standards are known. It is easier to be silent than to risk saying something the group will judge to be foolish.

We can make life a political game. As I write this chapter, political conventions are coming into play as an election year looms ahead. Political parties are putting pressure on candidates. Candidates are maneuvering and jockeying themselves to appeal to as many people as possible. They say different things depending on who is listening. Leaders are seeking ways to appeal to as many groups as possible. The political parties have become masters in using focus groups to determine where opinions are across the country, and what the majority is thinking. Rather than stating a policy, they echo the latest finding from their focus groups. Rather than answer a specific question, they move smoothly to standardized statements reflecting a safe preplanned position. Politicians stating definite opinions find themselves in difficulty. It is a risky place to be. Choosing this lifestyle produces non-committed relationships, shallow relationships, and no sense of real connection. A clear expression of self is lost as it tries to be whatever various groups require.

Dating relationships, and more committed unions, must manage pressure and tension brought on by the risk of being known. We want to look good in a dating relationship, put our best foot forward, make a good impression. It is very hard to share past failures, personal fears, or points of struggle when we have doubts about being accepted completely. The difficulty escalates, if we are dependent on having a girlfriend or boyfriend to have high self- esteem. In marriage, we can fall into the trap of being loved but unknown. Conflict in marriage can be especially painful. Sometimes it feels better to give in to a dominant partner than to face harsh words or other forms of rejection. I have seen women lose their identity to a domineering husband. I have seen men turn over all responsibility and fail to lead rather than take a stand, be known, and face rejection. It is easier to hide ourselves than risk losing someone on whom we are dependent. Being liked but not known is the easiest relationship to enter and maintain, but it has its problems. We lose something of ourselves, if we must conform to who others are. It is a very shallow relationship, and very empty.

KNOWN BUT NOT LOVED

We may be driven to take a risk if empty relationships dominate our life leaving us unfulfilled and feeling lonely.

If we feel alone, even when in a crowd, we may let ourselves be known. The risk is, as people know who we are, they can choose to shun us, neglect us, or disassociate themselves from us. Rejection is painful and pressures us to make a decision. We may decide to ignore who we are, try to fit in, and work to regain acceptance

Deitrich Bonhoffer ministered to his congregation faithfully. He spoke from conviction, but he lived in Germany when convictions were dangerous. He spoke about equality and dignity in all men. Germany in the 1930's was not a safe place to speak about such things. Bonhoffer defied the politics of Adolf Hitler, and paid with his life. Being known may not cost us our physical life, but it may mean the death of a relationship. It can feel equally as bad. It is hard to stand out. It requires strength. It requires that we know who we are. It is easier to take the other option, follow the crowd, and live life with acquaintances, or I can try to meet the need to be known through achievement. I can be known about.

Life can be lived as a sporting event. The goal becomes finding life's value and meaning by developing a fan base through fame and achievement. I will influence you to like me by knowing about me. It can feel like love, because you clap and cheer wildly when I am near. I will never forget what it was like for me in high school every Friday night. Our school had thousands in attendance. We were situated in a large city, in a state that went crazy every September. Football was king. I played on one of the better teams in the city, and when we emerged from the tunnel onto the playing field, the roar that went up also went into my soul. The feeling caused by that roar was exhilarating. We only had 10,000 people in the stands at a maximum. What is it like before college crowds of up to ten times that number? It can be addicting. I felt people liked me because I was on the football team. That is partly true. Some people did like me for that reason, but people did not know me. They did not like me or love me because they knew me. They knew about me! However, it was a substitute knowledge serving as a salve for the real need to be known. Fame is not love even though it may feel as powerful. Our world is filled with men and women striving for recognition and achievement, believing they are known and loved, because on the sideline throngs of people are cheering. I am saddened when I see people wearing their slogan tee shirts or "colors." Their sense of identity is wrapped up in a slogan, a group, or an idea and they substitute being known by being part of a movement. Some will destroy relationships in order to achieve. They would rather have a sense of value offered by fame. It is an empty existence, and one that can be easily lost even if one achieves the lifestyle of the rich and famous.

I have known others who appealed to the crowd seeking a sense of belonging, believing that people truly liked them. One class clown in my high school years was a brilliant student, but he occasionally found himself in tough situations he would rather have avoided. Because of the role he chose to play, he compromised himself in his search for love.

The number of young women today who get pregnant out of wedlock is staggering. They do not look to a crowd to belong but give in to the demands of a guy who seems to love them. I wonder how many of those cases can be traced to the desire to be loved. They are willing to give themselves away in the search for love, and as a result, face a tough existence.

Some choose to sacrifice love. For these, to be known feels significant. They may feel unlovable. The cost to be loved is too high. Some have suffered rejection and intense emotional pain. Many are talented or gifted enough to advance to responsible, powerful positions. Others may understand people and how to manipulate them. Their goal is reached through power. The thinking is I am unwilling to do things to please you. I cannot achieve what it takes to influence you to like me. Therefore, I will make you like me and do what I desire.

This option is demonstrated in dating relationships and in marriages. .Jealousy and control are dominant elements in the relationship, as one partner demands the attention and submission of the other. They remove any perceived risk of losing control. Managing schedules, limiting outside friendships or physical and emotional abuse are all tools used to diminish the one they wish to control. Fear has power, so threats are common. In the business world we often hear, "It is lonely at the top." For those who have used power to get to the top, it is not just a saying. If they have dominated and run over others to reach high positions, they do not have authentic relationships. They are known, but they have sacrificed love.

NEITHER KNOWN NOR LOVED

It is possible to bounce back and forth between seeking affirmation and conformity and risking being known. What happens when someone has tried a few times to be loved and never succeeded? What happens if from ones perspective he or she will can never risk being known? What if they feel unlovable and unable to achieve anything or be known for anything? This third scenario is the most damaging of the three we have studied. Those who know no love and are not known become dead relationally. They have no relationships, because they are numb to people. Killing emotions will remove the pain somewhat. Studies in recent years, made since the emergence of a number of serial killers, describe these individuals in sobering terms. They have no feelings for right and wrong. They cannot feel toward other people and have no sense of remorse regarding their actions. They are numb emotionally. They are often called loners.

I am describing the most extreme case when I talk about serial killers. There are others who have given up on relationships. They have ignored the pain or stuffed the pain below their conscious feelings. They go to the workplace every day, put in their hours, and return to an empty house. Perhaps, they return to a family and watch a television set until they fall asleep or go to bed. I have seen enough letters written to Abigail Van Buren to know this is not an uncommon occurrence. Men and women like these are pilgrims, living life in an emotional, relational vacuum. Whereas the serial killer allows his unknown silent rage to emerge in violent acts. These hopeless people bury their actions in apathy.

How can people go through life failing to love one another and know one another? It is not so much that we are not trying to know and love people. Rather, mankind has lost sight of what love is and what it means to know his fellow man. We have lost sight of the Creator who designed us to need these aspects of relationship. Having lost touch with Him, we have lost touch with ourselves and have looked for meaningful relationships in all the wrong places, and in all the wrong ways. Paul's words in Romans are correct in their assessment of our situation. Remember, it describes how this all developed when man refused to know God. In order to correct our faulty relationships, we must return to the God who designed the whole thing. But, can we really know God? Can we be sure the God we follow is not an aberration of the mind of man? I think we can!

Isn't it odd

that a being like God

who sees through the façade

still loves the clod

he made out of sod?

Ogden Nash

DAVE COLLINS

8

GOD'S PROVISION TO RESTORE RELATIONSHIP

He was content in his business, hardly noticing the comings and goings of the men in their starched shirts and tailored suits. The cautious looks, customary signs of respect, and intimidation did not register in his conscious thoughts. The precocious little boy was too busy playing between his daddy's feet. Little did it matter; his play area was under the most important desk in the world. John had no idea his daddy was the President of the United States. He was unaware to approach this desk, in this room, was a privilege enjoyed by only the powerful and influential. This was his daddy. That was all that mattered.

I remember seeing pictures of John-John Kennedy as a child in the White House. He was free to enter and roam about. It was his home. It was home, because his daddy was President.

There is a well- known photo showing John- John playing under the desk in the oval office. It is a powerful image of contrasts between young and old, power and innocence. Everyone recognizes it is President Kennedy at work. We all know it is the oval office in view. What a startling contrast to see a child at play in one of the most important few square feet in the world! Not only do we see a child at play in a serious chamber, we see the most powerful man in the world hard at work, at the same time, in the same place. What a contrast! How is it possible? It happened solely because of the love between father and son.

Can we alter the Kennedy photo replacing the oval office with the throne room in our Creator's heaven? Would we be allowed to play without concern at the feet of the Creator unconcerned about where we were, what we were doing, or who was working above us? Wouldn't it be odd, indeed, if God loved mankind enough to allow us that privilege and freedom? The Ogden Nash poem at the beginning of this chapter is one of the most profound statements I know concerning God's relationship to man, because it is like the snapshot of the two Kennedys. It clearly captures the remarkable separation in position and power between God and man while noting the close bond between the two. God the Creator and all-powerful One actually loves the arrogant little creature who is no more than a speck in the universe. He is truly like a sod of grass, totally helpless, and dependent on the Creator for its existence, alive one day and gone the next.

A BEING LIKE GOD

I have identified God simply as the Creator; however, He has revealed Himself to us in a number of ways throughout time. We must remember how utterly "other" God is from us. If we are in fact created, we have no chance at all of understanding this totally "other" Being. He is the designer and builder. The fact that we are made in His image and that He actually wants to have a relationship with us is our only hope of understanding anything about Him. No other created being, other than spiritual beings in direct contact with Him, can understand the significance of being in relationship with Him.

Our design and purpose reveal a great deal about God. God is relational. He designed a universe filled with creatures, one in particular, with which He could have relationship. He truly wants us to know Him and to love Him just as He knows and loves us. Consequently, He has taken special care to describe Himself to us revealing things we can understand about who He is. He has taken the initiative to relate to us. Otherwise, a relationship with God would never have happened, because we, like the rest of creation, are incapable of understanding Him apart from His desire to be known.

Some wonder how a sane person can make these kinds of statements regarding God. How can anyone ignore the philosophers, the mighty thinkers, the giants in human history? Brilliant men and women tell a different story about God, about man, and man's meaning in this universe. Mighty thinkers from diverse cultures have, over time, claimed to tell the truth about God in very explicit, definite, terms. It has been man's attempt to explain God and man from a limited human perspective. However, if one understands that God wants to be known, and has taken the initiative to make Himself known, it is reasonable to say He has found ways to communicate the truth about Himself.

Every culture has had its religious writings and customs. They have spoken about their god or the gods. However, only the Judeo-Christian explanation has the corroboration of history and experience. Written over centuries of time, in several different languages and cultures, the Christian Bible maintains remarkable and complete unity of thought. It is historically accurate, and has withstood multiple attempts to discount what it says about various peoples and events. God has demonstrated His power and sovereignty over His creation. He has provided a written record of who He is and what He desires in His creation. He has used a variety of people over the centuries to record all we need to know about Him. Though, it may try, modern science has not been able, nor will it succeed, in disproving what this word says about God.

Before the word was written, God had already designed a way to be known.

That which is known about God is evident within them for God made it evident to them. For since the creation of the world His invisible attributes, His eternal power and divine nature, have been clearly seen, being understood through what has been made, so that they are without excuse. (Romans 1:19,20)

Our conscience tells us God exists. Some have tried to discount the existence of God by pointing to ancient cultures and their various beliefs about God. They teach an evolution of culture in regard to their belief about God. They overlook the fact that all cultures believe there is a God. He designed us as Pascal says, "with a God shaped vacuum." God built man with the inner sense of Himself as part of the fabric of humanity. It would be more surprising to discover a civilization with no thoughts about a god.

That which is evident about God is within the heart of man. We have a conscience. We understand morality, that there is right and wrong. I can ask any crowd, at any university, if Hitler had any right to do what he did, and the crowd will say "no." Did he have the power to kill 6 million Jews? Yes, but power does not make a thing right. Had they done some unspeakable thing deserving of being extinguished? No. The majority of the German population did not oppose his actions. Does majority rule make a thing right? No. Hitler is remembered as a monster, because he broke a very clear moral law about killing innocent people. This moral law flows naturally out of the morality of the Creator. That moral law is written into the heart of man; therefore, the heart of man knows instinctively there is a moral lawgiver.

Man, however, has chosen not to believe the truth about God

teaching many opinions and descriptions of Him. He gave us eyes to see and a mind to think about what we observe in the cosmos. The cosmos itself points to a Creator. Its order is unimaginable. The intricacies of the NDA blueprints and the miracle of reproductions clearly indicate design. Design requires a designer; therefore, God says man is without excuse for ignoring the obvious. God wants to be known, and He built us to know Him.

We have the truth written in our hearts, but we have more. We also have the written testimony of people over thousands of years. Their testimony makes up much of our Bible content. The words of prophets describe God. They talk about His character, and His desire for men to live just lives. The testimony of men and women continues today in the lives of followers of God. They demonstrate changed lives, as a result of following God.

God spared nothing to make Himself known. He sent a letter of announcement; we call it the Bible. He sent messengers ahead to make sure people heard He would be coming. Then, He showed up in person. The man's name was Jesus of Nazareth, and He claimed to be God in a human body. He said He came to earth to tell people about The Father. Could there be a better person to describe myself to you than me? Of course not! I know what is most important to me. I know the important details you should hear, to know the real me. I am clearly the expert on myself. God has no flaws, so we can be sure His understanding of Himself is complete. Jesus had a discussion with a few of His followers reminding them of this fact. Here is their conversation.

I am the way, the truth, and the life; no one comes to the Father but through Me. If you had known Me, you would have known My Father also; from now on, you know Him, and have seen Him.

Philip said to Him, "Lord show us the Father, and it is enough for us."

Jesus said to him, "Have I been so long with you, and yet you have not come to know Me, Philip? He who has seen Me has seen the Father; how can you say, "Show us the Father?" (John 14:6-9)

Jesus explained to his followers, that in order to reach God, they must go through Him. He said if you observe His life, you will see exactly how God acts, how God thinks, and how God feels. He claimed to be God, and this conversation was all about knowing God.

The normal response of any person hearing claims such as these would be to say, "Get that person some counseling. They need help." Many said that to Jesus while He walked on earth. His response to them was to study His life; review everything He said and did; then make a rational decision based on the evidence they had right before them.

"Do you not believe that I am in the Father, and the Father is in Me? The words that I say to you I do not speak on My own initiative, but the Father abiding in Me does His works. Believe Me that I am in the Father and the Father is in Me; otherwise believe because of the works themselves. (John 14: 10-11)

Jesus was not a man who had lost touch with reality. He was reality. He knew His actions were consistent with His words, and that His words conveyed hope and meaning to anyone who would listen.

At this point in history, so far removed from the actual event, we hear people claim that over enthusiastic followers put words in Jesus' mouth after the fact. People still try to discredit the words of Jesus to remove the necessity of listening to Him and believing Him. There was no tape recorder present. Even if there had been, people would say it had been tampered with. No living person today can claim to be an eyewitness to the events surrounding Jesus' life.

I believe we do have accurate accounts of what He said, and what He did. Consider the implications of this statement.

"Men of Israel, listen to these words: Jesus the Nazarene, a man attested to you by God with miracles and wonders and signs which God performed through Him in your midst, just as you yourselves know. (Acts 2:22)

Peter, in an address before a hostile crowd soon after the resurrection of Jesus, is about to review the events surrounding the crucifixion. This statement was made to a crowd that included Jesus' enemies. One does not make this kind of argument, under these circumstances, if the claims are not verifiable and in order. He said, "As you yourselves know." What a powerful claim to the truth. There were no disputes at the time by those present regarding the facts we read in our Bible. If the resurrection had not happened, if a body could be produced, if anyone could have said, "No! What you are saying is false. Remember, it happened like this. Jesus never did what you say." They would have said it. They would have used whatever means possible to discredit or refute the claims of the earliest followers of Jesus. We can believe the things written about Jesus were accurate.

God can be known. He has written, sent messengers, and come personally to reveal Himself. The "Being like God" in the Nash poem is describable. We can look at the life of

Jesus and make many observations. Here are three.

GOD IS JUST

Some hard principles and abstract ideas are difficult to describe. A logical essay may not catch the essence of the idea. We can enhance a thought by telling a story or giving an analogy. Jesus, in His time on earth, taught many things. He talked about the Father, Heaven, the condition of man, and many other things. Often He used parables and stories to make a point clear.

One issue Jesus impressed on the Jewish leadership was their failure to lead the people under their charge. He repeatedly warned them that God had given them authority, but they were to represent Him in their life. They had turned from Him seeking selfish desires thinking God would not judge them, the children of Abraham. He warned them God is just, and does not overlook injustice and unrighteous living. God is a judge who will judge. He made his point to the Jewish leaders with this story.

Listen to another parable. There was a landowner who planted a vineyard and put a wall around it and dug a wine press in it, and built a tower, and rented it out to the vine-growers and went on a journey. When the harvest time approached, he sent his slaves to the vine-growers to receive his produce. The vine-growers took his slaves and beat one, killed another, and stoned a third. Again, he sent another group of slaves larger than the first. They did the same thing to them. Afterward, he sent his son to them, saying, "they will respect my son." But, when the vine- growers saw the son, they said among themselves, "This is the heir. Come, let us kill him and seize his inheritance. They took him, threw him out of the vineyard, and killed him. Therefore, when the owner of the vineyard comes, what will he do to those vine-

growers? They said to Him, "He will bring those wretches to a wretched end, and will rent out the vineyard to other vine-growers who will pay him the proceeds at the proper seasons." Jesus said to them, "Did you never read in the Scriptures, The stone which the builders rejected, this became the chief cornerstone. This came about from the Lord, and it is marvelous in our eyes. Therefore, I say to you, the kingdom of God will be taken away from you and given to a people producing the fruit of it. When the chief priests and the Pharisees heard His parables, they understood that He was speaking about them. When they sought to seize Him, they feared the people, because they considered Him to be a prophet. (Matthew 21:33-46)

There was no mystery as to the meaning of this story. God had given responsibility for the development of His kingdom into the hands of the Jewish leaders. He had sent messengers to make sure they did what was asked. The Jews had killed the prophets of the past, and now they wanted to kill the Son. Jesus made it plain God would exact justice on them. Justice is a funny thing. It is very easy to recognize and exercise, when we are the wronged party. Everyone cries for justice in that case. However, justice is the last thing we want when we are the ones who have done wrong. These were the religious leaders of the Jewish nation. Their job was to cultivate the spiritual lives of God's people. They were to guide men and women to a clear understanding of God. God would not turn His back, do nothing, and act contrary to His nature. It would be as great an injustice as ignoring the evil of theft, deceit, and murder described in the parable.

The United States has recently come to grips with the idea of justice. Following the 9/11 attack of the World Trade Center, an outrage that swept through the country. Thousands of truly innocent people died at the hands of a radical group of men acting in the name of their god. Not only had innocent people died, but children of all ages were left without mother or father. The cry rang out for justice. The act could not be ignored or downplayed. Justice demanded action. God, likewise, cannot ignore things done by man that are, in reality, horrible acts against the creation of God.

GOD IS POWERFUL

When we look around our world and see injustice and evil, our hearts yearn for justice. The world cries out for peace, but there is no peace. We see almost daily accounts of murder and bloodshed caused by evil men. We cry out and ask God for justice. "Where are you? How can you allow this to happen to innocent children? God, are you there?" The question slowly forms in the heart of man, "God either you don't care about justice and making things right, or you are unable to do anything."

We can observe Jesus in action, and understand God is indeed powerful. He gave testimony to the strength of God by means of numerous miracles demonstrating control over nature, time and disease.

And a leper came to Him and bowed down before Him, and said, " Lord, if You are willing, You can make me clean." Jesus stretched out his hand and touched him saying, " I am willing; be cleansed." And immediately his leprosy was cleansed. And Jesus said to him, "See that you tell no one; but go, show yourself to the priest and present the offering that Moses commanded, as a testimony to them.
(Matt. 8:2-4)

Leprosy was a mystery to the people of Jesus' day. It was a frightening thing because so little was known about the disease. It had a sure end... death. One difficult aspect of leprosy was its social consequences. In this culture, it had taken on a stigma. Those who suffered from leprosy were considered cursed by God, and marked by Him with this disease as a sign of His judgment against them. Those who contracted leprosy were ostracized from society. They were forced to live in colonies apart from family, friends and the rest of society. They were alone, as outcasts doomed to die in despair and loneliness. They were forbidden to touch anyone considered clean, on pain of death by stoning. Furthermore, they were required to give warning of their presence by yelling in a loud voice as they walked the streets..."Leper, unclean!"...pronouncing judgment upon themselves with their own lips, they were wretched, a danger to society, and not wanted.

They moved through life apart from anyone who could comfort or love them. What was this man feeling the day he heard Jesus was near? How long had it been since the last time he had held hands with a woman? Had he been married, and forced to abandon his family? How long had it been since the last embrace of a friend? Had he had any warm meals with friends in a room filled with laughter and camaraderie?

The man approached Jesus, risking death for coming so near. Jesus did not move away. Had the man heard of other miraculous healings? We do not know, but his statement is clear. "If you are willing," he said. The question in his mind was not Jesus' ability, but rather His desire. We cannot know the plans of God, why sometimes He acts quickly and decisively, yet at other times, He appears to be deaf or slow. It is definitely not a question of ability. This leper understood that fact. His question was like ours. Do you really care enough to act? Is there any surprise that the leper began the conversation with the statement "if you are willing?" Jesus' answer was simple, direct, and significant. He said, "I am willing." He said in those three words, "you matter to me, you are a significant person, you have value." What an amazing thing for the leper to hear!

Jesus demonstrated the power to change the course of illness, and restored this man's leprous body to perfect function. He did it right there on the spot, and he did it in a wonderfully sensitive way.

Some say God is cruel when He waits to respond. They question His character, implying He toys with us and is arbitrary. This account demonstrates the question of God's character is not the issue. Jesus demonstrated a character of compassion and love. He could have merely spoken a word and changed the course of this man's life, but he did much more than that. Jesus reached out and touched him. Here was a man deprived of physical human contact, lonely, and in need of a touch. Jesus not only healed a leper's infirmity by a physical touch, but by that same touch, healed the deep emotional need for human connection. Jesus looked beyond the simple cure to see the deeper needs. He was willing to touch a physical need, to put His hands on the sores and wounds. He touched emotional wounds that went far deeper than the outer layer of skin. This man received both a physical connection with Jesus and an emotional connection, but Jesus did not stop there. Notice Jesus told him to show himself to the priest. Here is a spiritual connection. The man would never forget Jesus healed him. He would also remember that Jesus pointed him to the spiritual connection he needed in life. It was the priests who were responsible for helping the nation connect to God. Jesus reminded him to do what the scriptures said to do. This was much more than "fixing" a man. The man felt loved and cared for. Jesus demonstrated by these kinds of acts that life is spiritual as well as physical, and He cares about both.

I do not know why God waits at times, but we have multiple examples of this same kind of compassion and care for people. He gave time to be with people. Rank and social status did not affect His relationships. He gave Himself away when He was tired, when He was hungry, when He was misunderstood, when nobody would know, but the one He helped. He guarded the dignity of people, and demonstrated a high regard for each person's individual value and worth.

Two things are evident in this miracle, and in all the works, He performed. Those two things are necessary for anything to happen. A person must have the ability to perform an act. Jesus, the Son of God, came to earth as God with flesh and bones. He was the visible expression of the invisible God proving by His works that God has the power to do whatever He chooses to do. His power was demonstrated in the ability to change weather, to change the molecular structure of water to wine, even giving life to the dead.

Secondly, to do good, one must have the desire to do good. Jesus told the leper, "Yes, you are important to Me, and I desire to see you well. That same heart is what always motivates God. It is a heart of love. It is at the core of His being, no less than any of His character traits. He cannot act contrary to His identity, and Jesus never did.

As we read the history of Jesus' life, many other characteristics show themselves. They are displayed in every day experiences not involving a miracle. He stopped to hear people, and connect with them. He stood beside the downtrodden and helpless. He offered comfort and wisdom. He gave of Himself offering forgiveness and hope to people of all social strata and importance. Crowds followed Him everywhere. They loved Him, and clung to His words, or they hated Him because His words revealed the darkness of their life.

We have evidence to disprove those false opinions. He was definitely not a weak person. He was courageous in standing against the current of power. He was winsome, and brought joy to everyone around. He had a personality that brightened the day bringing light where previously there had been darkness.

GOD IS LOVE

We have looked at two important character traits that help us know God. God is love. When we look at the life of Jesus, love was the overarching quality defining every moment of His existence and every action He took. Love was the motivating force sending Jesus to earth in the first place. Remember the verse we used to define love.

For God so loved the world that He sent His only begotten son that whoever believes in Him shall not perish but have everlasting life. (John 3:16)

Jesus came to earth, because He saw the state of man. We are in desperate trouble. We are dying and without hope. He has come to rescue us. Love sent Him here to accomplish that task. Love sustained Him throughout the ordeal. Love is what gives us life today. There is no greater love possible than the ultimate act of Jesus on earth. His death on a cross, at the hands of men, is the center point of all history, because no greater love has ever been demonstrated in all of history. We will understand the depth of God's love when we see what God saw when He looked down at man.

THE CLOD MADE OUT OF SOD

If you are a mom or a dad, you have been through the drill. We, as parents, know babies must grow up. They must learn how to take care of themselves, feed themselves, and dress themselves. There are times when I get worn out making sure these things are covered in my own life. No one plans to feed and dress their 40-year-old son or daughter? Apart from illness or another catastrophic event, we know such a lifestyle would be unhealthy for everyone involved. So, we prepare our kids for life. We teach them how to do the simplest things first, then move on to more and more complicated tasks until that glorious day they can do things for themselves.

In route to their maturity, there will be a day like the one I experienced with my son. He was very young, so we were in the beginning stages of the process. It was the pouring milk into your own glass stage. He had seen me do it a hundred times. I am not sure what goes on in the mind of a child, but pouring milk became a fascinating sport to him. It was something to conquer. Maybe it is the same feeling I get pouring a little golf ball into a hole in the earth. Aaron began asking for the milk, and as I poured, he put his little hands on the condensation soaked milk jug.

"I help," He said. At one point, he felt ready to pour the milk by himself and changed the "I help" to "I do it."

Trouble began. His concept of "I do it" did not match the reality of the situation. His muscles had not developed enough to physically handle the weight of the milk jug. His coordination enabling him to manipulate liquid into the glass was even less developed. You know the story. One day he took it upon himself to pour his own milk. He picked up the full milk jug, or rather tipped it. He sort of hit the glass with the milk, tried to overcompensate for the quickly escaping milk, knocked the glass over, and spilled the milk all over his plate. That upset him causing him to drop the milk jug to the floor emptying a gallon of milk all around our table.

What is going on in this scenario? A child is attempting to do what he is incapable of doing by himself. It is not a bad thing. He simply cannot do it without the help of his parents. There were consequences. There was a mess to clean up. You may be smiling as you remember a similar episode in your house, or your own similar attempt. A smile is fine in this case, but what if the task at hand is more serious than filling a glass with milk? What if the consequences affect lives, or possibly destroy lives?

God created His universe, and chose to make one of His creatures special. He created His "Children." He made us in His image. It was all part of His plan to have a huge family of children, with whom He could share love and life together. Everything flowed out of whom He was, and was consistent with His own goodness and order. Man's part was to trust Him, allow our strength to come from Him, and obey Him for everything to function, as it should. We do not have the strength to manipulate our world, or pour our lives without spilling them, into whatever situation life presents. We do not have the coordination to manipulate the pieces where they are intended to go. We cannot see how things need to be in the future. We do not understand, or learn from our past. Our present is hit or miss. All this comes, because we say, "I do it."

We previously looked at the origins of our independent thinking. Our very first parents chose not to believe God. They chose to believe they could be like Him. They were like little children believing they were capable of doing something they could not do. They disregarded the warning by God that this choice against Him would have consequences. So, like little children, they spilled the milk.

Unfortunately, their spill had drastically more profound consequences than milk on the floor. They brought on death for themselves, and their descendants. They caused a break in their relationship with God. Without His guiding and sustaining strength, they could not handle the weight of life and lost touch with their very selves and with each other. Men and women have not changed since their first destructive choice to ignore God. We have more technology and scientific knowledge, but our relationships still suffer. Our world is still witness to the inhumane treatment of women and children, murder, every kind of atrocity by man against man, and self- inflicted horror. Instead of cultivating the earthly garden given to us, we are destroying it.

Can the problem be fixed? How can we clean it up? To answer that question we must go back even further than the garden experience to uncover the source of the problem.

How you have fallen from heaven, O star of the morning, son of the dawn! You have been cut down to the earth, you who have weakened the nations! But you said in your heart, I will ascend to heaven; I will raise my throne above the stars of God, and I will sit on the mount of assembly in the recesses of the north. I will ascend above the heights of the clouds; I will make myself like the Most High. Nevertheless, you will be thrust down to Sheol, to the recesses of the pit.

This is a description of one of God's angels. He was known as "star of the morning." Obviously, he was a thing of beauty with great power. This being had a change of heart, and became known as Satan. He was the serpent we saw in the garden talking with Eve. Do you see the argument? He thought, "I will make myself like God." I t is the same argument he gave Eve.

What is "to be like God?" We have talked about God being

the Creator and Sustainer of the universe. He has many attributes theologians have discussed for centuries. He is everywhere. He knows everything. He is all-powerful. He is completely and totally independent of all things, and everyone. He needs only Himself and that is enough. To say I will be like God is to say that I don't need God or anyone else. I am complete within myself. I will make all my decisions based on my own thinking and choosing. I will do as I choose. I will act when I choose and where I choose. I will be the center of everything.

You will notice Satan said in his "heart" he would do these things.

This is a heart issue. Our first parent's hearts were, at one point, centered on God.

They both listened to Him, and were content with Him. They found joy in obedience, and found life fulfilling and complete with God at the center. Their hearts changed when they chose to be like God. Their hearts turned inward and died. We all have this heart problem. It cannot be fixed by our efforts. We need a new heart, because the old heart has been lost. We need a heart inclined toward God, because the hearts we possess now point inward. We have lost our hearts. They are like a compass that cannot find north. We have no reference point to direct our lives. Consequently, we lose our way in life. It all begins with a lost heart.

We must face our ultimate problem, lost hearts. With lost hearts, we have lost a relationship with our Creator as loving children He also loves. Our relationship with Him is lost leaving us to fend for ourselves, precisely what we sought when we chose independence. Unfortunately, since we have lost touch with God, we are incapable of managing our own lives or relationships with our fellow men. We are delusional, because we still think we can make things right. We still think we can do it. We are lost and don't even know we are lost. Or, if we do, we erect facades of grandeur, self-aggrandizement, the accumulation of goods, power, popularity, and whatever means we believe create the appearance of a successful life. We think, all the while, we are living life as it was meant to be. This is the problem Jesus came to fix.

HE SEES THROUGH THE FAÇADE AND STILL LOVES

By the mercy of God, mankind is able to feed itself and care for itself. However, the deeper issues of the soul, and the resulting casualties in relationships, are at the mercy of circumstances. Our relationship with our Creator God is severed. There is nothing we can do about it. From our point of view, we have no need to do anything about it. There is no desire to change, because we still want to be like God, independent of all constraints.

God calls this desire to be like Him, independent of Him, sin. He says there is a consequence for sin. The consequence is like a wage paid for labor done. Our wage for sin is death. We have to face a physical death, our soul's separation from its body. We also have to face death spiritually, our soul's separation from God. God has prepared a place for those souls to reside far away from Him. He cannot do anything else, and remain true and consistent to Himself. Justice demands the evil choices receive punishment. His holiness cannot allow any stain of sin to enter marring His own perfection. It would be intolerable for Him.

I have a very strong conviction honesty is an indispensable character trait for a righteous person. I, therefore, determined years ago, my word would be true, and I would have an indisputable reputation for honesty. Most of the time, this has been a straightforward manner of life without a great deal of cost. However, there have been times when honesty has cost me pain and anguish. I have had to admit guilt or failure rather than take the easy way out of a situation. I could not honestly make an excuse or tell a half-truth. No one who makes a phone call to my house will ever hear me in the background saying, "Tell them I'm not here." If I allow these small "white" lies to become part of my life, I will know the truth. I will have killed a part of myself, and lost my honesty. If God allows any kind of sin or wrong behavior to be a part of His world, He will lose part of Himself. He will not, and cannot, let that happen. He will, therefore, judge all sin. Honesty is a serious issue for me, yet I must admit some failures. God will never fail. His moral perfection will never be compromised.

In being true to Himself, God has not overlooked His incredible and extravagant love for us. We are the apple of His eye. He cannot think of us without love. He is crazy about us. He cannot ignore that core part of Himself any more than He can ignore His righteousness and holiness.

Returning to John 3:16, we know God is still active. His love is true, not waiting for us to respond or show any signs of desire for Him. He has taken all the initiative toward restoring us to life and to a relationship with Himself. "God so loved the world that He sent." He has come to us. He was and is aware of our deep need and overlooks the facades we erect to hide our lostness, and deadly destructive ways. His love compelled him to act and pay whatever price needed to meet our need, to pay the wages we owe for sin, to restore us to life, and to restore our relationship with Him. The cost was staggering. Jesus had to come to earth ......and die.

I have watched the movie, "Saving Private Ryan, a number of times. The story of bravery and the noble character of men who actually fought and experienced the kinds of events depicted in the movie inspire me to think beyond myself. I come to the end of the movie watching the never say die attitude of Captain Miller as he was bleeding to death amid the rubble that was a town before the war. He is shooting his revolver at an advancing tank when the help they had been waiting for arrives. Ryan goes to him as Captain Miller is taking his last breaths, and listens to the barely audible whisper from the man who came to save his life, "Earn this", whispers Captain Miller. It sounds so appropriate and normal. Men had given their lives for the sake of this one man. Shouldn't he do something to merit that great cost?

The most amazing thing about God's love is that He never asks us to earn anything. He knows we cannot pay enough. We would never be free of the guilt we carry. He has taken it upon Himself to do everything necessary for our rescue. It is staggering what Jesus did and what He accomplished by dying on a cross and rising to life out of the tomb. Look briefly with me at five theological words. This is what God did. He ignored our façade of self- sufficiency and lovingly did everything necessary to give us a new heart, a heart destined to live rather than die.

Jesus provides a new heart by means of His death and resurrection. Mel Gibson produced a movie depicting the events that took place at the death of Jesus. The Passion of The Christ does not hold back in graphically presenting the gruesome nature of crucifixion, the form of death Jesus suffered. His body was covered in blood as a result of the wounds suffered before He was nailed to the crossbar of the cross. We see His trial and the anger of the religious leaders who clearly did not accept the words of Jesus or believe He was truly the Son of God. They believed He was crazy, dangerous, and needed to be put out of the way. The Roman soldiers had done many crucifixions. Their attitude was anyone convicted of a crime worthy of this form of death deserved the harsh treatment they got. Any charlatan who claimed to be king over their emperor deserved especially harsh treatment. Furthermore, after having done so many crucifixions, they became hardened to the blood and the cruelty of the moment.

In the final moments of the movie, we see Jesus leaving the tomb alive. It is only a brief moment, but it is the most important moment. Thousands of people have been tortured and bloodied over the centuries. They have suffered tremendous pain, and undergone unthinkable treatment, but none have ever died, and then walked out of their grave ...except Jesus of Nazareth. The fact that He came back to life is the clearest validation that what Jesus said about Himself was true. His death was more than another execution carried out in human history. This was the Son of God dying for the purpose of rescuing lost men. He did it, motivated by an extravagant love that would pay any cost to have a loving relationship with mankind.

Here is what His death accomplished.

RECONCILIATION

The death and resurrection of Jesus reconciled man to God. What does that mean? Why is it important? When one is reconciled, there has been an accumulation of debt. Then, the debt is covered. It is paid, and the debt is forgotten. It no longer exists, and in effect, it creates a fresh start. Reconciliation can describe an economic situation, or be applied to people and their relationships.

Southerners in the United States have a deep sense of what

happens to relationships because of debt. I heard growing up, "Don't get "beholden" to anyone." It was as if everyone was trying to outdo the other by kindness. At times, it was very difficult to accept a kindness, because that kindness put the recipient in an indebted position. The recipient would owe their neighbor. The situation changes from I have to pay my neighbor back, to how will I pay my neighbor back, to can I pay my neighbor back? Go to a restaurant and observe groups having lunch together. What happens following the meal? How many times do you see a near fight break out, because someone grabbed the check? No, you can't pay for this! It's my turn! Give me that check!

Then, with a swift flick of the arm, the check is stolen, and tucked away in a pocket removing all chance to for anyone else to pay.

What happens when a debt is incurred between people? The relationship changes. For the one who owes, it becomes a burden that somehow grows with time. The debt has not been paid, and there is an emotional compounding of weight. It feels like a weight, something heavy placed on the heart. I'm letting that person down. I'm not a good person. It's like I have stolen something from my friend. I'm worthless. I can't do anything. I can't even pay back my friend. I don't want to see my friend, because I know, and I know they know we're not "even." There once were debtor's prisons. People with a debt were placed in prison to force the debtors loved ones to pay. Sometimes, it can feel like we are living in a prison without bars when our emotional debts have accumulated to a breaking point.

For the one owed the relationship changes as well. Over time he may wonder, "Why hasn't my friend paid me what he owes? Does he care about me? Was he trying to take advantage of me? Can I really trust him as a friend? Is he my friend at all?" Debt tends to sever relationships especially over a long period of time.

Imagine the greatest debt you owe. Is it a house payment, college loans, business debts? Those debts are insignificant to the greatest thing anyone can possibly owe. Have you ever considered that you owe your very life? Anything physical we owe simply goes away when we die. We do not get to play with things anymore, at death; we do not take them with us. We do not have to worry about how to pay for our toys or anything else when we leave this world. We have noted the wages of sin is death. In effect, we are accumulating a very real spiritual debt to God that one-day must be collected. We owe Him our life. God says He created us as eternal beings. We may die and be separated from our present body, but our spiritual self- lives on. That spiritual person carries a real debt into eternity. Is it any wonder, then, that we have such a hard time being close to God? We have a heavy burden to pay. Our debt creates enmity between God and us. It separates us.

The debtor can pay a debt personally, or a substitute may pay. When our son got his driver's license, we made a deal with him. We said, "We will help you keep the car's upkeep, help you with gas, but there is one thing we will not do. If you get a ticket, you have to pay." We wanted to discourage irresponsible behavior. He knew there would be consequences to irresponsible driving. He would have to pay. Thankfully, this never became an issue, but I did wonder, sometimes, when he was out at night. How far would I go for him? What if he got a ticket he could not pay? What if he was sent to jail and have a record follow him throughout his life? In that case, I think, I might pay the ticket for him. I would be reconciling him to the State. Another word to use is "atone." I would be atoning for his actions. That is what God did. He has paid our debt by assuming it Himself. He has atoned for our sin in our place. The bible says it like this.

He made Him who knew no sin to be sin on our behalf, so that we might become the righteousness of God in Him. (2 Corinthians 5:21)

For it was the Father's good pleasure for all the fullness to dwell in Him, and through Him to reconcile all things to Himself, having made peace through the blood of His cross, through Him, I say, whether things on earth or things in heaven and although you were formerly alienated and hostile in mind, engaged in evil deeds, yet He has now reconciled you in His fleshly body through death, in order to present you before Him holy and blameless and beyond reproach.
(Colossians 1:19-22)

Jesus Christ paid my debt to God. He became a substitute for me personally, and since I owed God my very life, Jesus gave up His own. God now declares publicly, "You owe me nothing. Your debt is cleared, and now you can start fresh with Me."

PROPITIATION

And He Himself is the propitiation for our sins; and not for ours only, but also for those of the whole world. (1 John 2:2)

Joe came home from school every day not knowing what to expect. He was the black sheep of the family, and seemingly could do nothing right. Mom had expectations that Joe look and act a certain way, but it was not him. His mind loved to explore and go outside the box. He wanted to be different, dress different, go off the beaten path. Mom could not handle a sideways glance of her neighbor friend when Joe pulled one of his stunts at the grocery store, or had any problem in school. The family had other difficulties, and of course, it was easy to see that Joe had to be at the bottom of the issue. It was his fault. Joe's dad, an alcoholic did not help matters as he joined in on blaming and accusing. He paid for the multiple counselors, and counseling sessions meant to "fix" Joe and make him be what he was supposed to be. All the while, Joe's parents failed to see their own failures. Joe's sense of self was dead, and he began to think death might be the best thing for him. Joe finally got some proper treatment, and began to get handles on life. He had earlier begun a relationship with God, and given time, he began to experience health in his life. He is now married, and has a wonderful relationship with his wife. However, all is not well with Joe. He has completely severed all ties to his mom and dad. Meanwhile, they have changed themselves. They have recognized some of the hurts they inflicted on Joe, and they are sorry. They love their son, and miss him. They have tried to call, but no one will pick up the phone. They have written letters apologizing, begging for some way to be reconciled to Joe. The problem is, for Joe, they cannot do enough. His hurt and pain cannot be atoned by his parents, and he can never be "satisfied." His parents cannot be propitiated. They cannot do enough to earn his forgiveness. Even though none of the parties is perfect, they have changed. There is still a wall preventing this family from helping each other experience the love they all desire.

God is satisfied! We do not have to do anything more for God. Unlike in the movie Saving Private Ryan, we do not have to earn anything. God is completely satisfied. He is not mad at us. He does not have any problem with sneaky little thoughts creeping back into the corner of His brain warning Him about us or reminding Him how much we owe.

There is no more burden of sin debt for us. It has been paid in full. God sees the receipt of our payment every time He looks at Jesus. It is enough, and He is satisfied!

JUSTIFICATION

Imagine yourself at trial. You are the defendant. The judge sits high behind his imposing bench looking very serious, holding power to destroy your life in his hands. All arguments have been made, and you are commanded to rise for the judge's decision. "Not guilty," He says. With loose knees, you wonder if you will fall over. You find yourself involuntarily exhaling, and are surprised to discover how much you had breathed in, and how long you had held your breath. Suddenly, you smile, laugh uncontrollably, and turn to hug somebody. Anybody will do, your happiness and joy is so full. Haven't you seen this very thing acted out in real life? There have been a number of high profile trials over the last few years, and it always seems the same. We feel the tension as the defendant rises. It seems forever before anything happens, and then, following a favorable judgment a scene much like the one I have described plays itself out.

To be pardoned, or declared "not guilty", is an amazing thing. Before the verdict, all the weight of doubt presses down. All the arguments have been made. All the evidence is in. The future is totally in the hands of another person. One is entirely helpless standing before the judge. Nothing more can be done, and the defendant's future rests in the hands of the one in power. All he can do is wait. The consequences flowing out of the judge's mouth forever impact the one standing before him. The greatest hope of the defendant is to be "justified."

What does it mean, and what are the consequences? Before the declaration of not guilty is ever heard, many things have taken place. A crime had to have been committed. Someone or a group of people became suspects, and evidence was collected. That evidence had to be sufficient to point to the person or persons now on trial. They were arrested, placed in jail, and came to trial. In effect, they have become enemies of the state. Their freedom has been removed. Other people make decisions when they will eat, when they will sleep, and most other decisions directing that person's life throughout the day.

The declaration, "not guilty," removes all guilt from the crime from the person who had been charged. He is free. He is able to walk out of custody, and resume life as a free person. He has no guilt placed on his head. He has nothing to pay to the state. He has no further consequences or damages to pay in his life associated with the crime committed. It is as if he were never charged.

Not only is he no longer associated with the crime, he is restored to good favor with the state. He is a citizen in good standing, and recognized as a valuable member of society. He freely associates with all people, and has no fear of being accused again for this crime. Everything offered by the state, and available from the state, is now accessible again. He is free to be productive, and build a legacy in his life. The restoration to good standing gives meaning, purpose, and value back to the person in question.

We must keep in mind the judge, assuming he is an honest judge, is the one who pronounces and declares the pardon. He is the one who has the power and the position to weigh the evidence. He has the authority to make the decision. He simply examines the case before him, and impartially makes a decision based on the evidence before him. His decision is called to be just and proper. In fact, if he does not judge impartially and justly, the whole system will fall apart.

Society will fall to anarchy, power seeking, and vigilante justice.

If the system is working, the defendant has no power to influence the decision of the judge. He cannot promise to do better in the future, because he is being judged for something already complete. He cannot promise to give the judge anything special, bribe him with favors or anything else, because a good judge must impartially look at the facts. The defendant cannot ask the judge to weigh his whole life against the one act in order to be pardoned for that act. The one act is in question, and the judge must look only at this case to determine guilt or innocence on this one matter. Truly all power rests in the hands of the judge.

The defendant standing before the judge is you and I. The Judge is God the Father. The most astounding fact is God clearly and loudly proclaims, "Not Guilty!" His judgment is not based on the fact we truly did not commit a crime against Him. The evidence is clear and overwhelmingly strong against us. He does not give pardon by weighing our lives on a balance with the good on one side and the bad on the other. There again, we would lose. He does not judge based on the hope of our improvement or any promise by us to do better. His judgment is based purely on what we have already discussed. Jesus Christ died on a cross and spilled His blood as atonement for us. God does not pronounce us guilty, because the punishment has already been paid. We have been atoned, and it is enough.

Nevertheless, knowing that a man is not justified by the works of the law but through faith in Christ Jesus, even we have believed in Christ Jesus, so that we may be justified by faith in Christ and not by the works of the law; since by the works of the law no flesh will be justified. (Romans 2:16)

Therefore, we have peace with God. We are restored to good standing in His kingdom. Our knees should buckle, and our joy should overflow. We should be able to sing and dance just like David did thousands of years before Jesus showed up. He was looking forward to being justified by God.

How blessed is he whose transgression is forgiven, whose sin is covered! How blessed is the man to whom the Lord does not impute iniquity, and in whose spirit there is no deceit!

When I kept silent about my sin, my body wasted away through my groaning all day long.

For day and night, Your hand was heavy upon me; My vitality was drained away as with the fever heat of summer.

I acknowledged my sin to You, and my iniquity I did not hide; I said, "I will confess my transgressions to the Lord," and You forgave the guilt of my sin.

Therefore, let everyone who is godly pray to You in a time when You may be found; surely, in a flood of great waters they shall not reach him.

You are my hiding place; You preserve me from trouble; You surround me with songs of deliverance.   (Psalms 33:1-7)

REDEMPTION

Mother Ryan is in her apron by the kitchen sink. Through the window, she looks out on open fields stretching to the horizon. It is a beautiful summer day. A breeze is blowing, and it is peaceful in the house. She is alone preparing the family meal. We watch with her, while down the fence line, a black limousine slowly makes its way up the long drive to her house throwing out a cloud of dust behind it. Soon, she will be on the front porch as the uniformed men hand her the letter with the most dreadful news any woman can ever hear. Her sons, away at war, have been killed. Three sons are gone, and now she has only the youngest left. We feel with her as she sinks to her knees in despair, and we easily identify with her hurt and anxiety over James, the one son still alive.

That is the basis for the movie Saving Private Ryan. A family had lost three of four sons. The last needed to be found, and returned to his home to carry on the family. It is a story of redemption. The word means, "to tear loose." James was in the thick of battle in danger of death on a daily basis. He faced hardship in a land he did not know, exhausted, hungry, and sleep deprived much of the time. Those he fought spoke a different language than he. Redemption has the idea of a "ransom" being paid. In this case, seven men were sent to find James, and almost all paid for his life with their own. They were a ransom paid to rip him out of battle.

We talk about stories of redemption in which something of value is rescued or drawn out of a bad situation. It could be a person who has wasted their life in worthless pursuits. It could be a good character quality that surfaces in the life of one in which you would not expect to see good. There is always deliverance from something bad. It could be a bad situation. It could be a bad life. It could be a bad investment. Usually we think of being delivered "to" something else. In the case of Ryan, we see him at the end of the movie desperate to know that his life had been lived well.

In every case, there is a cost. We have a saying in our house.

You get what you paid for. We believe, if a thing has value, it will have a corresponding price. From opposite perspective, we say it like this. If it sounds too good to be true, it is probably too good to be true. So, when we think of redemption, we think of the price paid, and compare the value of the thing being redeemed to the cost. In history, we know cases of famous children being kidnapped and offered for ransom. I recall the Lindberg case. Historically, it is a famous person or someone with means to pay who is asked to "buy back" their child.

At the cross, Jesus paid the ransom price on our heads. It was his life. He bought us back with his life, and delivered us from death. He rescued us from an old life of sin to a life of beauty. He redeemed us from being enemies of God, and gives us citizenship in the Kingdom of God. Ultimately, He redeems an evil heart that does not want to know God, and gives us a pure heart with the ability and the desire to love God and others wholeheartedly. This new heart understands itself, and from it flows righteousness and goodness. Remember, our problem is a heart problem.

Being justified as a gift by His grace through the redemption, which is in Christ Jesus whom God displayed publicly as propitiation in his blood through faith. (Romans 3:24-25)

Christ redeemed us from the curse of the law, having become a curse for us – for it is written, "Cursed is everyone who hangs on a tree" – (Galatians 3:13)

Jesus "bought" us back with His blood, because it satisfied the justice of God. It is a gift we did nothing to earn. God took the initiative. He did what was necessary to satisfy His own love for us, and exact justice for the sins committed by man.

No wonder the cross is the center point from which we measure time. God loved the world so extravagantly…..He did send His son to die for us. In doing that, He broke through and continues to break down our façade of self-sufficiency. He opens the door for a renewed relationship with Him. This is what He has always wanted, His children enjoying His company while He enjoys theirs. He wants to make the picture of you and me playing contentedly at His feet as natural and real as the picture we have of the son of the President of the United States playing at his feet.

He wants to see us functioning with each other as we were intended. We can now know one another at a deep level, and love one another as we were designed. Now it is possible for the deepest longings of our hearts to be met.

I cannot close this chapter without making the greatest offer ever made. It is the same offer that has been made to man from the beginning. I accepted the offer over 40 years ago. Now I present it to you personally by way of the words in this book. This is it. Jesus Christ died so you can have life. His death and resurrection satisfy the justice of God, the love of God and everything in between. He offers you the opportunity to choose. Who will you follow…yourself or Him? It is a choice recognizing that God is God, and He deserves our complete allegiance and trust. He is our Creator. It is a choice recognizing the truth of our personal guilt for ignoring God. It is a choice to give Him His rightful place in our life. It is a choice that recognizes the incredible mercy and love that God has for us. It is a choice that recognizes our complete dependence on Him. We simply say to God we chose to accept His gift of eternal life made possible by Jesus. We trust Jesus' death and resurrection were enough to satisfy God, and we now place our complete confidence and trust in Him for our lives from this moment on. It is an act of telling God we will let Him have our life rather than continue trying to run it ourselves. We will trust Him, beginning now, believing He will take care of it forever. It is very simple yet very profound. What is your choice?

9

THE CONNECTION
GOD KNOWS US

It truly is an amazing thing to say the Creator of everything both knows us and loves us. However, that is the marvelous truth. To say God knows us is, perhaps, more palatable than to say He loves us. After all, God is seen as the all-powerful and all-knowing One. It does not stretch the imagination too much to say He knows us. Most religions hold to some sense of their god knowing people. Yet the question can be asked, "What do you mean by "know?" Is it a personal thing? Is it like the knowledge I have of historical figures? Is it simply an intellectual thing, like knowing how something is made or how something works?

I have known in my lifetime 11 Presidents of the United States. I can make that statement, and be completely truthful in the sense that I know their names, have seen them on the television, would instantly recognize their photo or even recognize their voice. However, in one sense, I have not known a single President. I have known about them. In some cases, I know a great deal about them having read their biographies and lived through the historical setting in which they impacted my life. The difference is I never made personal contact with a single one of these men. There was no personal connection.

There is an altogether different kind of knowing. I remember the first time I saw Sharon Brecht. I was attending University. Every university has a meeting place, or someplace near campus, where students gather. One day I entered the student center during a break between classes. It was a habit of mine to go to the same little corner of the cafeteria. I was part of a group of young men and women who had become friends over the course of the year. We liked to meet at the student center to eat, share stories, and play cards. There, seated in the familiar group of girls and guys, was a new face attached to a petite body. She instantly caught my attention, because she was laughing constantly giving life to the conversation at her table. She had bangs that curled just above her large dancing eyes, and every time she laughed, the curls bounced as if to accent the humor in her words. I was caught. I do not know how many times I saw this enchanting woman before I learned her name was Sharon. I found out she was my age, was not dating anyone, and that she was a fun person. At this point, I still only knew about Sharon. Only after I sat with her, and played cards with her, did the relationship move from a non-existent possibility to a reality. We began dating and spending more time together. We did all kinds of things together, and learned a great deal about each other's likes and dislikes. We discovered some truths about our family backgrounds, all the while sensing a growing attraction. Today, she is my wife, and no human knows me better than her.

The development of our relationship has progressed now for over 40 years. It all began with a chance meeting where the possibility to connect changed everything. Connection is key to all relationships. Without connection, they simply do not exist. Not only is connection necessary to begin a relationship, it is essential for growth in relationships. Without connection, people never move beyond knowing about one another to actually knowing one another. We do not move beyond being acquaintances without spending some time together sharing our lives and experiences. As we entered the dating phase of our relationship, the connection and commitment between Sharon and I grew stronger, and we had opportunity to know each other more deeply. We allowed one another to know the little secrets tucked deep within our souls; only the trusted few are allowed to know. We actually wanted to share those things. The day we married, the connection was sealed. The Bible says we became one. I not only know that from an intellectual standpoint, I know emotionally. The final connection between Sharon and me means she has first-hand access to every part of my life. We experience life together as one. We know how emotions move one another and what kinds of things go to the center of our souls. We know each other physically completely. We can tell when something is wrong, or when we don't feel well. I sometimes recognize symptoms of an illness in Sharon before she is aware she does not feel well. People laugh when we complete each other's sentences. We are also impacted by each other's spiritual life. Our common reliance in our Creator affects our relationship in every way. He is the same person we both follow and listen to; moreover, our common relationship with Him moves us closer to both Him and each other.

I have a question. Since humans need connection points to know each other and have a relationship, do God and man need connection points. Is it even possible to use the word "relationship" with God? After all, God is so totally "other" than us, it seems impossible to relate with Him. How can we communicate with one another? How can we possibly understand the emotions of God? How is it possible for God to want a relationship with us? After all, we are only a small part of His creation.

I create paintings, but there is nothing within me desiring a relationship with a painting. Why would He stoop to be in relationship with us any more than he would the rocks and the trees?

Truly, the most amazing thing I know is this, namely that

God actually wants to have a relationship with us. If you were to boil the Bible down to a single theme, it would be the God who made everything, has done everything, to make a relationship with Him possible. It is all about God creating us to have a relationship with us, how we broke the relationship, what He did to restore the relationship, and our eternal future together. The reality about God is He has personality. He is not a force or a philosophy. Because He has personality, He wants to be known, and He wants to know us as persons. The Bible tells the story of a God with personality. It claims within itself to be the very breath of God, autobiographical. It is His story about Himself and everything He created. He thinks and feels and He is able to speak. He wants to communicate and share Himself. That is why we were created. We were made in His image, different from all the rest of creation. God uses relational terms when referring to us. He talks about us as His children. He calls us His bride. He talks about His deep, relentless, and extravagant love for us, and He talks about knowing us.

Every religion I know outside of Christianity recognizes the enormity of the difference between God and Man. They do not talk about man having a relationship with God. They speak of man serving God or appeasing God. They talk about what man must do to keep God happy or to manipulate God to bless them. Others elevate man to equality with God, but these religions do not recognize God as the all-powerful Creator and Sustainer of the universe. Others reduce God to some kind of "energy", empowering life. His personality is removed, and without personality, it is impossible to have a relationship, communication, or love. There is no connection without personality. There is no "knowing." There is just existence, two sticks lying on the ground, or pebbles scattered around a stream. It truly is monumental to consider the possibility of relationship with God apart from the fact that God Himself has taken the initiative to help us understand this startling truth. He has done everything possible to help us know Him.

God took the initiative in every aspect of our relationship with Him. Following creation, He walked with Adam and Eve in the garden communicating with them. They refused to obey God, and generations followed who chose not to know God. God did not give up. He continued to speak to man through prophets and the written word, ultimately coming as "The Word" in Jesus Christ.

Who, although He existed in the form of God, did not regard equality with God a thing to be grasped, but emptied Himself, taking the form of a bondservant, and being made in the likeness of men. (Philippians 2:6-7)

He did all this to connect to man even though man did not understand. The God of the bible connected with His creation when He entered that creation, not as the all-powerful God who made it, but as a part of creation. God knows man, because He became a man. Not only does He know man as a man, He has demonstrated His incomparable love for man as a man. God's act of becoming man allowed Him to know us as one of us while helping us to know Him as He truly is. When God put on flesh and bones, He connected to humankind in at least three ways. These three points of connection are exactly what we need to grow relationally. They are physical connection, emotional connection, and spiritual connection.

PHYSICAL CONNECTION

Physical connection is the most basic way to know another person. It occurred between Sharon and me when I sat with her, and introduced myself. She saw me and talked with me. As our relationship grew we moved to physical touch, holding hands and kissing. Jesus Christ was fully man. He emptied Himself of all He had as God in Heaven. Jesus experienced everything you or I expect to experience in our lives. It began with His human birth experienced exactly as every other human, and ended with His death. Every physical aspect of life was lived out by Jesus. Consider the chronicle of His life.

Matthew, Mark, and Luke all record a forty-day fast by Jesus as He began His public ministry. They acknowledge He became hungry John records:

He came to a city of Samaria called Sychar, near the parcel of ground Jacob gave to his son Joseph. Jacob's well was there. So Jesus, being wearied from His journey, was sitting by the well. (John 4:6)

Not only was he physically tired, He knew thirst and asked for a drink of water. On the cross he said, "I thirst." Jesus' physical body functioned like our bodies. Its nerve endings were fully active. He felt what we feel, and His organs operated according to the physical laws of the universe. His brain was like ours, so His thoughts and understanding came through the same sources as ours. His physical development and function was completely human. He followed the normal course of growth, or as Luke says,

He grew in wisdom and stature. (Luke 2:52)

His life ended in a physical way due to the trauma suffered by his body through the beatings and suffocation on a cross. His pain was real. It was the normal pain associated with torture inflicted by crucifixion. Why didn't God place a computer chip within us filled with all the information we need to know about Him and connect the chip to our brains? He could have ended all confusion among humans as to the existence of God, His character, His desires, and all other aspects of the divine. He could have eliminated all religious wars and conflicts. He could have done any number of things to "wire" correct information into human beings. If God chose to "wire" us with complete knowledge of Himself, He would have remained apart from us and unloved. He would have eliminated relationship. He gave us a choice to listen to the witness of the visible universe, and to our conscience. He took on our physical form to connect to us relationally. He is not totally "other" simply demanding our obedience or programming our obedience. He entered our physical world to know us, and for us to know Him. He experienced life like us and understands our place in the universe from a physical perspective. We have the ability to see God. We can hear His words and communicate in a personal way. Those who walked with Him touched Him, and felt His embrace just as He felt theirs. Because God chose to lessen Himself by taking on a physical body and walk in time and space, mankind experienced a knowable, personal God. What's more, God knows us physically totally apart from anything He could have experienced as God. He knows our physical pain, and the course of life making His connection with us complete.

EMOTIONAL CONNECTION

Jesus could have visited our earth taking on a physical body while maintaining all His inner character as God. In other words, He could have visited our world without having to face the emotional hurts, feel the emotional pain we feel as human beings, or understand any emotions humanity feels. In that case, He could not know how it feels having to make a choice between good and evil. He would not understand the struggles we face in our souls, in the core of our being. He would not be in touch with the feelings that bubble and sometimes explode out of our soul. He would not truly know us, and our knowledge of Him would be mechanical. Yet, God did not choose to come to earth clothed in Himself, totally other, and unapproachable. He experienced everything as an emotional human with all the feelings of a human. (Heb. 1:18) Human experience is so completely tied to our feelings and emotions that God chose to allow Himself to face every emotional aspect of life in the person of Jesus Christ. He was not a spiritual apparition or a robot. He was a feeling person. He empathized with the people of His day. Human emotions have not changed over the course of time. He can equally empathize with us, and understands us completely. One can examine the life of Jesus and see He lived the whole range of human emotions. Consider a few examples of how Jesus connected with us emotionally.

Not much has been written about the childhood of Jesus. We have enough information to know He grew up in a loving family, and He knew what it was to submit under His parent's authority. Joseph, his father, was a carpenter. Jesus was known as the carpenter's son, and was a carpenter himself. Following the culture of the day, Jesus entered the profession of his father. He grew up in the shop watching his dad cut wood and fashioning the furniture. He learned to do the things his father did, experienced frustration making his own mistakes along the way, and learned the practice of his trade. Jesus had to deal with frustrations in the learning process. He knew the joy of hearing praises for a job well done, and the pain of hearing corrections for work needing improvement.

We who have brothers and sisters have been in situations where competition rather than encouragement was the norm. There is generally competition between siblings. We often compare ourselves with each other each trying to make our place in the family. We want to get the biggest piece of the pie. We want the best spot. I have had to be the referee more than once as my children yelled from the back seat of the car, "He's on my side!" or "She's touching me!"

I remember a football game I played in junior high. My sister, who was one year older than me, came to the game to cheer for our team. She is very competitive, and got into the game emotionally. Her voice was persistent and strong. It was loud, and I recognized it above all the other screaming moms and dads circling the field. It penetrated my conscience deeper than the intimidating voices of my coaches, especially when she was negative.

"Why did you miss that block?" Can't you do better than that?"

Those kinds of words cut right to my core. I was hurt and angry. I wanted my sister, more than any person there, to say good things about me and be proud of me. I wanted her encouragement more than anything. She was my sister, after all. I wanted, even more, to hear great words from my parents. They knew me best, and had the power to affirmed my worth and my abilities more than anyone else. Words have power, especially when they come from significant people. To hear something negative from them was a heavy blow. They, more than anything else in life, gave me an indication as to where I stood in the world. Was I any good? Did I have what it took to be a man? Was I lovable?

Jesus had to deal with the same kinds of family issues we all face between brothers, sisters, moms, and dads. He had to deal with conflict and lack of support from His siblings. He came to earth with a difficult message that ran against the current thinking of the Jewish leadership. He spoke to hostile crowds, was criticized by them, and had to demonstrate the truth of his words. Not only was his message difficult, but His claims about Himself were hard to swallow. He said, "The Father and I are one," claiming to be God. He claimed those who believed in Him would never die. He claimed He could give life. Two thousand years of history does not change the reaction of people to those who claim to be God. They have been, and are viewed as unbalanced or insane.

We have two instances where Jesus' brothers and sisters appeared to side against Him. Matthew records an account where Jesus spoke to a large group of people including the religious leaders. Jesus began condemning those leaders. He called them snakes, and said they were evil, and were going to face judgment from God. They said He was the devil. In the midst of these kinds of claims and accusations, the tension and emotions were running high. In the middle of this tense situation, someone came to Jesus with news His mother and brothers were outside wanting to talk with Him. (Matt. 12:46) Nothing is written about what they wanted to discuss; however, we have a later story that may shed light on this case.

John records an incident in which Jesus says, *"I am the bread of life. Your fathers ate the manna in the wilderness, and they died. This is the bread, which comes down out of heaven, so that one may eat of it and not die. I am the living bread that came down out of heaven; if anyone eats of this bread, he will live forever; and the bread also which I will give for the life of the world is my flesh." (John 6:48-51)*

From our perspective, long after the statement was made; it does not seem so difficult. We understand He was using figurative language. However, we can guess the thoughts of those who heard the statement.

"What is he talking about?"

"Is this man advocating cannibalism?" "He has got to be crazy!"

"What in the world does he mean about living forever? That is impossible."

"He has lost his mind."

From our present day perspective, we believe Jesus was talking about offering His body as a sacrifice for sins. His flesh was going to be offered up as a kind of food. Bread was the staple for their diet. They would later understand He was talking about being the source of life. Just as we eat bread and it is absorbed into the body to become the source of energy, regeneration, and life, so would Jesus' life be in a spiritual sense. He was offering Himself as the spiritual staple for life that does not end with physical death.

Following this discourse, many of Jesus' followers left him. They did not grasp the spiritual implications of the message and probably thought Jesus was insane. Later, Jesus' brothers approached Him suggesting He go to the feast of booths in Judea. It would have been dangerous for Him to go, because many of the leaders wanted to kill Him. Take note how John describes their actions.

Now the feast of the Jews, the Feast of Booths, was near. Therefore, His brothers said to Him, "Leave here and go into Judea, so that your disciples also may see Your works which you are doing. For no one does anything in secret when he himself seeks to be known publicly. If you do these things, show Yourself to the world." For not even His brothers were believing in Him." (John 7:2-5)

I can see sarcasm dripping from their suggestion. They were saying the same things the religious leaders were saying.

"You are making some pretty big claims here, Jesus. Why not take advantage of the feast? You know every important person will be there. You should go and do some of your miracles. Prove yourself. Come on. Don't waste your chance." It appears they had given up on Jesus and were mocking him. I wonder if their attitude began earlier when they interrupted his teaching. (see Matt.12) Were they embarrassed by Jesus at that point? Had they come to take him away? Did they progress from a place of trying to take care of their strange brother to a place of openly mocking him? Whatever the family attitude happened to be regarding Jesus, their actions, and words had to sting. Jesus knows knew how it feels to be criticized, misunderstood, and mocked by the people who knew Him listened to his teaching, walked with him, and saw his life first hand. Add to that the misunderstanding and mocking from those who should have loved him the most, his family, and we get a glimpse into the emotional struggles Jesus had to deal with.

Jesus knows another emotion associated with family. He knows loss due to death. I have been fortunate to have never lost a parent or child, but if I live, it will happen. I know the loss of grandparents, but their death cannot compare to a loss of mother, father, spouse, or child. We all face it at some point. Jesus, the everlasting One, the Creator, came to earth as one of us and knows how that feels. Joseph, Jesus' earthly father, is described in some detail at the beginning of the gospels. He was an honorable compassionate person. I suspect he was a wonderful husband and father. He was part of the narrative when Jesus was 12, but was not mentioned again. Mary and Joseph are not discussed together apart from Jesus' birth and the incident during his 12th year. We hear of Jesus being the carpenter from Nazareth. He had assumed his father's trade, and possibly his business. It appears that Joseph was gone. Since he did not abandon her when Mary disclosed her pregnancy before their marriage, there is no reason to believe Joseph ever left her. Most assume he died sometime after Jesus was 12 years old.

When my son was 12 years old, I was dying. I had lost weight and was getting very weak. One day I collapsed. I went to the doctor and had blood work done. Indications were I might have pancreatic cancer. One doctor thought I would be dead within a year. My family reacted normally with anxious thoughts and worry, but my son showed his anxiety in unusual behavior. He began staying out with his friends as late as he could, and avoided being home. He was gone all the time, and rarely spent time with me. It was his way of coping with the possibility I was going to be gone soon. He did not know how to handle it, so he coped by living as if I were already gone. I wonder how Jesus handled the death of Joseph? It had to be difficult and painful, losing a parent at a young age, a good father, one who loved him.

With the death of Joseph, Jesus became the head of the family. He assumed financial responsibility for his family. He, therefore, knew at a young age, the pressure and responsibility of being the provider for a family.

Even though it appears the family of Jesus did not understand Him, there is no evidence to believe they abused Him. Yet, there is great evidence Jesus experienced all kinds of abuse, the most obvious during His death. Crucifixion was an abominable way to die in its physical torture, but also because of the stigma attached to it. Roman citizens, by law, were not crucified. It was reserved for the worst of criminals, and was used as a way to demonstrate the power of Roman law. Knowing one would be seen by everyone outside the city gates, hanging in shame, nearly naked, on a cross was emotionally excruciating even before the physical torture began. Adding to the shame of being crucified, having seen other crucifixions, one anticipated with dread, what was coming physically.

For three years, Jesus taught the truth. He gave Himself completely to the task of saving His people. Yet, from the beginning, He was mocked by the very ones who should have understood and helped Him spread the message. They tried to trap Him in speech, turn the hearts of the people against Him, and silence Him any way they could. They attempted to stone Him. The teachers and Jewish leaders were the ones who arranged to have Him crucified, and stood at the base of the cross mocking Him saying such things as "He saved others; let Him save Himself if He is the Christ."

I can imagine the pain of watching an apartment building burn down with all the people inside. How much more pain would I feel if I had seen the fire and run to each apartment trying to warn people. What if some yelled at me for disturbing their sleep or took a shot at me with a shotgun to run me off? How would it feel if some laughed at me or called me a lunatic just before dying in the flames I was trying to rescue them from?

It is definitely difficult to experience rejection, but how much more difficult is it to experience abandonment? Jesus felt both. When He was arrested, His twelve closest friends all ran. Peter, one of His closest friends, said three times within Jesus' hearing, "I don't know that man." It was the night Jesus was arrested and stood trial for things He did not do, being accused of leading people away from God while trying to lead them to God. Peter had acknowledged Jesus was the Christ, yet this night his desire was to distance himself from the truth teller....his friend. Jesus had already felt the pain of going through a difficult time alone. That same night He had asked his friends to pray with Him, and three times, He returned from His prayers to find them asleep. He was in agony that night as He prayed alone. Peter denied Him, and the next day He hung on a cross surrounded by those who were glad to see Him in agony.

Jesus connects with us emotionally at every level of pain, but also in joy. His humanity was complete. The need for friendship, love, purpose in life, laughter, joy, and every need of a human soul, were part of Jesus' human experience. He experienced friendship, laughter, and companionship with His twelve disciples. Over a three-year period, they walked together through His homeland. He played with children, enjoyed the celebration of a wedding, shared the joy of people healed from diseases and oppression, shared meals with friends, and as a carpenter, experienced the joy of creating. Jesus experienced deep affection and gratefulness as Mary washed his feet with her tears, and dried them with her hair. I wonder what joy He felt as a different Mary sat at his feet listening to his teaching and growing as a person. She believed in who He was and in what He was saying. He knew the love of a mother as Mary wept at the base of the cross, and He knew the devotion of a friend at that same moment, seeing John there beside His mother.

Jesus knew how it feels to fight injustice and evil. He knew what it was like to get angry, to take action, and to see things stay the same. We have the account of His entry into the temple where true worship was to happen. Yet, the leaders had allowed people to set up businesses within the temple, the place meant for worship. Jesus became so angry He turned over tables and drove people out of the temple. He did that on two occasions. He knew what it meant to be persistent in the face of frustration.

There were no shortcuts in the life of Jesus. He lived completely. His life was complete emotionally. He suffered physically and emotionally. He loved, and was loved deeply. He knows how we feel in the deepest part of our souls.

Spiritual Connection

The human experience is not complete without a spiritual connection. Atheists notwithstanding, every culture on earth has had a spiritual component. The understanding that God exists is built into our DNA. Every culture has grappled with who that god is, what he is like, and what he wants from us.

In order for Jesus to relate to us on the spiritual level, He must connect with us spiritually just as He did physically and emotionally. He had to grapple with the same spiritual questions all men ask. Jesus knows the spiritual journey of man. He knows what it is like from the human perspective to seek God and grow spiritually. Some people mistakenly believe that Jesus, because He was God's son, had the same spiritual powers as God has. However, Paul makes it clear in Philippians 1:7-8 that He abandoned his Godly prerogatives, and took on our human character completely.

"He emptied Himself, taking the form of a bond-servant, and being made in the likeness of man. Being found in appearance as a man, He humbled Himself by becoming obedient to the point of death, even death on a cross."

The reality is Jesus, as a human had to grow spiritually. A spiritual journey parallel to our own characterized his life.
Jesus learned obedience, which is at the core of spirituality. Remember our whole problem with God began as an act of disobedience. Every culture is searching for God, because rather than trusting Him for guidance and life itself, we have chosen to trust ourselves and go our own way. We have lost touch with who God really is, but we have not lost the

understanding that God is out there. Disobedience caused the break in relationship between man and God, and obedience is the answer to restoring the relationship.

For as through one man's disobedience the many were made sinners, even so through the obedience of the One the many will be made righteous. Romans 5:19

Jesus did not come into this world ready to be its savior. He had to grow up thirty years before setting out on His ultimate mission. He had to grow in obedience as part of His spiritual journey.

Although He was a Son, he learned obedience from the things, which He suffered. *And having been made perfect, He became to all those who obey Him the source of eternal salvation. Hebrews 5:8-9*

His journey in obedience began early in life. At age twelve, His parents took him to a feast in Jerusalem according to custom and discovered on their way home Jesus was missing. After a frantic search among the relatives, they went back to Jerusalem to find Him. They found Him in the temple asking questions of the religious teachers and debating with them about God's work on earth. Luke records the reunion very realistic sounding terms.

His parents basically asked, "What were you thinking? What are you doing? Don't you know we have been frantic over you?"

Jesus' response is very telling. He said, "Didn't you know I had to be in my Father's house?" He also told them something like this, "You should have known where to find me all along. This is why I am on earth."
We could guess that Jesus won the argument, and continued

on with His mission. However, Luke says this:

But they did not understand the statement, which He had made to them. And He went down with them to Nazareth, and He continued in subjection to them; and His mother treasured all these things in her heart. And Jesus kept increasing in wisdom, in stature, and in favor with God and men. Luke 2:50-52

Jesus, like us, learned how to submit to His Heavenly Father. In the same way we learn submission, He submitted to His earthly parents. That submission continued for 18 more years.

Not only did Jesus learn obedience through submission, He practiced spiritual disciplines in order to know God the Father and learn what He (Jesus) was asked to do. The Gospels record numerous occasions where Jesus rose before dawn to pray. His disciples often woke after Him, and did not know where He was. It was still dark when He went out to pray. After feeding thousands of people, Jesus sent his disciples away in boats while He stayed behind to pray. Before major decisions, we have record of Him praying all night. He prayed before selecting the twelve who would be called His disciples. He was praying on the night he was arrested and tried. The Gospels say, "it was His custom" to go to the synagogues on the Sabbath. He went to the festivals and feasts of the Jews practicing the things God had asked the nation to do. Jesus knew the scriptures well. He practiced fasting, even one recorded fast of forty days.

On his forty day fast, Jesus experienced the same spiritual battles all humans face. He was tempted to disobey God. The Gospels record the devil tempted Jesus with three things. They were to change rocks into bread, to jump off a high cliff, and to worship Satan. These temptations were not new. They are, in fact, basic temptations everyone must face in different degrees every day. John describes the temptations this way:

For all that is in the world, the lust of the flesh and the lust of the eyes and the boastful pride of life, is not from the Father, but is from the world. 1 John 2:16

Every temptation in life falls under one of these categories. We will be tempted to feed our physical pleasures in ways God has not authorized. These are lust of the flesh. Things like over eating, pornography and drunkenness falls into this category. Lust of the eyes drives us to want things. Materialism falls under the second. We envy and seek to have something for the wrong reasons or at the expense of others. The third is power, called the pride of life. We want to be in control and have power over others. We are arrogant, boast, and put others down. We seek raw power. These temptations are at the core of our spiritual battle, because every human is prone to choose one of these paths to get what they want rather than trust God to give what is needed. It is our way of taking control of life, and being like God rather than being subject to God. Jesus' temptations fit into the same three categories. He could have quenched His physical hunger, which had to be huge after a 40 day fast. However, by making rocks turn into bread, He would have misused power to do it. He could have sought a pride driven rescue by jumping off a cliff. I suppose He was pretty low emotionally after wandering around a desert wasteland 40 days. It would have been nice to be pampered and be told, "You are too valuable to get hurt." He showed tremendous restraint in rejecting the offer to control all the beautiful places on earth after eating dust 40 days.

Examine the first instance of the temptations. It is recorded in Genesis. Eve was walking in the garden with her husband, Adam. God had told Adam not to eat the fruit of one tree in the garden, and it happened they passed by that tree one day.

The same tempter Jesus would face years later came to Eve and said something to the effect, "You know, Eve, God has been holding out on you. The reason He doesn't want you to eat this fruit is that He knows it will make you like Him. You don't really have to be subject to Him. It is your choice. You can be just like Him and do whatever you want. Just eat this fruit."

Eve put up a half-hearted fight and said, "But God told us not to eat it...or even touch it." Then she continued the conversation with her own observations. This fruit would be good to eat. (Lust of the flesh) It certainly is a beautiful tree. (Lust of the eyes) It is a good thing to be "wise," and the tree can do that for me. (Pride of life)

Eve lost the battle. She ate and gave it to Adam who also ate. We have been eating the same stuff ever since. Ever since our first parents believed the lie of Satan, we have followed their exact pattern. I believe this is at the root of the relational games we play involving knowing and loving one another. The lust of the flesh leads us to believe our need for love can be met through our senses. The lust of the eyes leads us to believe what we see is what we know about others. What people can see in us is good enough. The pride of life leads us to believe fame or power is the most important thing about being known. We believe through power and control we can manipulate others to love us, or if we have power we will not need love.

Jesus could have, like every other human, chosen to do what He wanted, but He chose to obey God instead. He knows what temptation feels like, but He also knows the truth. His spiritual journey carried Him all the way to the cross. At that point, Jesus had withstood every test. He was "one" with the Heavenly Father, but He was about to face the hardest test of all. He knew the cross was hours away, and began to pray for God to remove the cross from his journey. Can you blame Him? Knowing the physical torture He was about to endure would be enough to make anyone squeamish. He knew about the emotional pain accompanying the cross, but His greatest anguish may have come as He realized the spiritual cost of going to the cross. He knew God's justice would be poured out on Him for all mankind. On the cross, He would face the full wrath of God the Father. It was an incredible weight to bear.

I consider my life, and the length I will go to help someone. Death and facing the wrath of God would be too much for me. I believe I would die for my wife or my children, perhaps for my family, or someone as close as a brother. Then I consider my enemies. Most often, I do not even want to offer them my time. I would not consider going to a cross for an enemy. That is the spiritual battle Jesus faced. It is what God wanted. Jesus was deep in prayer as He considered His choices. His words tell the story of His spiritual journey. They show His strength and what is equally possible for me to do. He asked for God to find another way, but He concluded by saying, "If this is the way You choose, I will go." This is the true spiritual side of all mankind. Originally, that is what both Adam and Eve told God. Whatever you want is what we will do. It is the goal of our human spiritual journey now.

On the cross at the peak of His suffering, Jesus displayed another side of humanity's spiritual life. Jesus was dying. God, the Father, had abandoned Him, because He had taken on the worst part of humanity at that point, our sin. Even then, Jesus said, "Into Your hands, I commit My spirit." At the darkest hour, when God seemed completely out of the picture, Jesus chose to trust Him. Jesus put Himself in the Father's hands with complete trust that His God would do good. At that point, Jesus displayed the ultimate spirituality of man, and the truest test of our faith.

We began this chapter talking about the magnitude of the statement that God loves us and knows us. Everyone wants to be loved by God. Why would we want Him to know us, and know as one of us rather than as the all-knowing Creator?

Remember the story of the little boy who lost his hand. A stranger broke through all the fear and doubts of a little boy's heart, because he had experienced the same fears and struggles the young boy was facing. To break through to the human heart, it took someone who could say with all honesty, "I know what you are going through. I know how it feels. You can make it."

God knows us as we are. He has experienced everything we face as humans. He speaks to our hearts with an understanding heart. He connects at the heart level, because He knows. Jesus has set the standard for how to build deep relationships. It must begin with knowing. He came to earth as one of us to know us completely. Furthermore, He came to Earth as one of us, to love us completely. Jesus came to earth as one of us to also show us how to know and love others well. .

"Example moves the world more than doctrine."

Henry Miller (1891-1980)

"Personally I do not resort to force - not even the force of law — to advance moral reforms. I prefer education, argument, persuasion, and above all the influence of example."

Rutherford Hayes (1822-1893); 19th U.S. President

DAVE COLLINS

10

JESUS - OUR EXAMPLE

I stated earlier Jesus came to this earth to restore a broken relationship between God and man. Mankind has refused to know God as He is. Rather, we have made up our own concepts of what God is like, and played at religion. Until we know God, it is impossible to love Him, and therefore impossible to have a real relationship with Him. The amazing thing is that God continues to love man deeply. He knows and loves us as our Creator, and through His son, Jesus. Jesus has made it possible to have a very real relationship with God, and is the perfect example for us to observe and understand how to know and love God, ourselves, and others. Jesus said so Himself.

Consider this example. On His final night before being arrested and sent to the cross, Jesus was with his twelve closest friends giving final instructions. John records these words:

Do not let your heart be troubled; believe in God, believe also in Me, In My Father's house are many dwelling places; if it were not so, I would have told you for I go to prepare a place for you. If I go and prepare a place for you, I will come again and receive you to Myself, that where I am, there you may be also.

"And you know the way where I am going. "Thomas said to Him,

"Lord, we do not know where You are going, how do we know the way?" Jesus said to him, "I am the way, and the

truth, and the life; no one comes to the Father but through Me. If you had known Me, you would have known My Father also; from now on you know Him, and have seen Him." Philip said to Him, "Lord, show us the Father, and it is enough for us. Jesus said to him, "Have I been so long with you, and yet you have not come to know Me, Philip? He who has seen Me has seen the Father; how can you say, 'Show us the Father'? "Do you not believe that I am in the Father, and the Father is in Me? The words that I say to you I do not speak on My own initiative, but the Father abiding in Me does His works. "Believe Me that I am in the Father and the Father is in Me; otherwise believe because of the works themselves.

Jesus told telling his disciples they have access to God. Jesus has prepared a place for them in Heaven. He said by knowing Him, they know who God is and what He is like. He told them plainly with His words, but He also lived a life demonstrating those words were true. His life was open to scrutiny, and was consistent with all He said. His life showed us that God knows us and loves us. He lived a life completely open and honest. He was willing to be known. He lived a life sacrificial in its love for the people with whom He had contact.

He lived a perfect life in relationships, and built a bridge to relationship with God. Consider how his earthly relationships demonstrated His desire to know and love people. Jesus came to heal, but He did more than simply fix infirmities.

I have had surgeons who were like auto mechanics. I would drop my car off at the repair shop and tell the mechanic its symptoms. He suggested things that might be wrong, and told me he would take a look. He called later with a solution and a price asking if I wanted to do the repair. Later, I would pick my car up, and know nothing more about the mechanic than that he was proficient in his job. Some surgeons have treated me exactly like an automobile. I have gone in to the doctor's office and discussed my problem. Spasms of pain in my back were keeping me up at night preventing me from doing things I wanted to do. The doctor took x-rays, and told me I needed surgery to take out bone spurs and free the nerve in the spinal column. We set a date. I had the surgery. All is well. Today, I can't even remember the surgeon's name.

I know another doctor who is my friend. Our families have known each other since he was in medical school. We have cried together over a crisis. We have laughed and played together. We have loved each other's children, and prayed for one another. He was a spiritual mentor for me in my early days of following Jesus. There is a huge difference between this doctor and the back surgeon. Both are proficient in what they do. They have good reputations, and I am confident in their abilities. However, there is a level of trust in my friend Jack I have not given to any of my other doctors. I never question his motives. I know he may make a mistake, because he is human, but he will never be negligent or take advantage of me. He is actually the reason I went to the back specialist. Jack told me it was time.

In the same way, Jesus is more than a surgeon merely fixing our problems. He really knows us and truly loves us. Remember the leper and how Jesus touched him to heal the physical disease without overlooking his emotional pain. Jesus helped him think about his spiritual needs as well. Later in this chapter, we will see examples of Jesus affirming a woman who had been rejected for 12 years. He protected a little girl from the pressures and discomfort of a crowd. Jesus was a healer at every level, physical, emotional, and spiritual. He is the example we can follow as we seek to live life the way it was designed to be lived.

It is important to note that Jesus never took advantage of His power or His fame. Jesus' popularity and fame certainly grew as people heard about blind people seeing, sick people getting well, and dead people coming back to life. There were skeptics, but there were those who wanted to cash in on His fame. Jesus could have cashed in Himself. Had Jesus succumbed to that human tendency, He would not have loved in purity. We would ask the question in every circumstance, "What was He after? What was in it for Him?" There would be serious doubt about His authenticity. We would not know God, and we would be left hopeless. However, His love was pure. He saw the needs of people, and met those needs without asking for something from them. He never sought power or prestige. He simply loved as we have defined it. His constant message was that all He said and did were those things he saw His Heavenly Father doing.

If you know Me, you can know Him, He said. I am reminded of the famous writing, "One Solitary Life."

He was born in an obscure village, the child of a peasant woman. He grew up in another obscure village where he worked in a carpenter shop until he was thirty. He never wrote a book. He never held an office. He never went to college. He never visited a big city. He never traveled more than two hundred miles from the place where he was born. He did none of the things usually associated with greatness. He had no credentials but Himself. He was only thirty-three. His friends ran away. One of them denied him. He was turned over to his enemies and went through the mockery of a trial. He was nailed to a cross between two thieves. While dying, his executioners gambled for his clothing, the only property he had on earth. When he was dead, He was laid in a borrowed grave through the pity of a friend. Nineteen centuries have come and gone, and today Jesus is the central figure of the human race and the leader of mankind's progress. All the armies that have ever marched; all the navies that have ever sailed; all the parliaments that have ever sat; all the kings that ever reigned put together have not affected the life of mankind on earth as powerfully as that one solitary life.

Amazing. Consider the opportunities Jesus had to take advantage of his fame. John tells us of one instance when the people were going to take Him by force to make Him their king. (John 6:14-15) He had just fed 5000 people with a couple of fish and five loaves of bread. This large crowd had all experienced a miracle. They were excited about Jesus, and felt like He could set them free from Roman occupation. They were looking out for themselves. It would have been very easy for Jesus to take advantage of the moment, but He did not. Just as He had turned down Satan's offer for power, Jesus never took power offered by anyone. He realized the people were going to take Him by force to make Him king, so he slipped off into the mountains to be alone.

Just as Jesus never accepted offers of power, He never took advantage of the privileges that come with fame. Privilege tends to make us humans smug. For example, I mentioned going to a doctor's office earlier. I have to admit, there have been times when I was a little angry by the time I got in to see the doctor. Some have a policy of putting you at the back of the pack if you arrive late for an appointment, yet they have no qualms about having you sit one or more hours after your appointment time before letting you in. I quit going to one doctor for this very reason. He was smug about his position.

As Jesus progressed in His ministry, and His name began to

grow, He could have taken on that kind of smug attitude. Men with power, men in authority, approached Him. He was known as the Healer, and many were asking if He might be the Christ. That kind of notoriety never changed His love for all people. He never confused status with human value. One day, Jairus, a local synagogue leader, a man of power, approached Him with an emergency. He pleaded for Jesus to come heal his very sick daughter. It turned out the little girl had died while Jairus went for help. Here was an official with some power, who was very stressed, imploring Jesus to come. I can imagine the anxiety he was under and the temptation to exert power to get the help his daughter needed. Crowds always seemed to form wherever Jesus went, slowing Him down, making it hard to move quickly. That is exactly what Jairus discovered as he approached Jesus.

The crowds were pressing in, and jostling everyone. One desperate woman was there, but as a woman in this culture, she would not have been given the courtesy to be near Jesus. The men would have that honor. Pushing her way forward with a sense of urgency, she managed to reach out and touch his outer cloak. She had suffered twelve years, had spent all she could, and gone to everyone she could to get relief from her suffering. Here we see a desperate poor woman, a nobody, reaching out in what probably felt like her last chance to be healed.

To everyone's surprise, Jesus stopped and asked a very unusual question. "Who touched me?" I wonder what Jairus was thinking when Jesus stopped for this woman. I wonder if he was tempted to apply some of his power to push Jesus past the moment. What kind of question was this, anyway, in the middle of an excited crowd of people all trying to get close to this famous person? Jesus had sensed a difference in her touch, and was willing to stop in spite of the pleas of the synagogue official to hurry. It turned out to be a poor woman, yet He took time to converse with her and hear her story. She was not a person of leadership or importance. She was just a poor little woman. He cared for her and gave her dignity regardless of her station in life. She could have walked away from that crowd with nothing more than a healed body. I'm sure she would have been overjoyed with that, but Jesus gave her more. He stopped just for her. She was important enough for Jesus to encourage her and praise her for her faith. She left with much more than physical health restored. Her soul was also bolstered. She knew Jesus cared for her personally. She knew that her faith mattered.

As Jesus spoke with the woman, news arrived that Jairus' daughter had died. Jesus could have turned his attention to others at that point. Instead, He told Jairus not to worry and that His daughter would be healed if he believed. Jairus having just seen a miraculous healing of the woman still needed the encouragement of Jesus. Jesus told him not to fear. When they arrived at the home of Jairus, they encountered another crowd. Loud and chaotic, they crowded around Jarius' home. They were all wailing and crying over the death of the little girl. There were those who genuinely cared for the family and hurt with the family. Many were there putting on a show.

Jesus made another strange comment like the one he made about being touched in a crowd. . He said, "You can stop crying. She's just asleep." They laughed at him. I'm sure they were all thinking something like "we know when someone is dead. You haven't even been here. How can you tell us she's just asleep?" I think it is interesting that Jesus limited the number of people who entered the dead girl's room to His most trusted disciples and the mother and father. Why would He do that? Could this have been another demonstration of pure love?

If a large group had been allowed in, and seen what happened, all the attention would have been placed on Jesus. They would have been praising Him and focused on another great healing. By keeping the group intimate, Jesus allowed a mother and father to hug their little girl without any distractions. The girl was spared all the embarrassment, and endless questions and talk of so many people. She was able to freely receive the love of her parents. This was a tender act of insight on Jesus' part. In the span of a very short time, Jesus demonstrated pure love to both ends of the social spectrum. Love was the issue. It is always that way with God. He is not moved by power, prestige, or personal accomplishment. He simply loves people.

There is another kind of person to whom Jesus showed love. The embarrassing person. We all know them. They say the wrong things at the wrong time. They draw the wrong kind of attention to themselves, and make everyone feel uneasy. They don't dress right. They are awkward and hard to be with socially. We have an account of this kind of person in Jesus' life. He was a poor man, a beggar. He was blind, which added to his embarrassing position. His name was Bartimeaus.

We encounter Bartimeaus doing what he always did. He was begging on the side of the road. The road he had chosen this day happened to be the path Jesus had chosen. Beggars cannot be very successful if they are unaware of their surroundings, unaware of who might be near, or unaware of a potential gift. Bartimeaus was paying attention to his surroundings. Even though he could not see, he must have heard as the crowd approached. Crowds are never quiet. I wonder if he asked questions about the approaching crowd. Was it one that could give or one that might sneer at him?

He began to make inquiries and discovered this was a crowd following the teacher and healer, Jesus. He had heard of this man. The stories about him were all over town. Many were saying Jesus was a fake and just a crazy man. Others were saying he was the Christ. We know Bartimeaus believed the latter, because he got excited. He began to yell out loudly, "Jesus, son of David have mercy on me!" His was not a gentle cry. He wanted to be heard above the crowd.

Some of Jesus' followers heard the loud cries. It began to wear on them. He was too loud, too obnoxious. They tried to quiet him down, but nothing worked. Bartimeaus was not going to miss his chance. He shouted more and more loudly, and more specifically, "Son of David, have mercy on me!" This guy was disturbing, so they tried harder to quiet him down. He asked His followers to bring Bartimeaus forward. It did not matter to Jesus how he looked or how he acted. This man desperately wanted to be helped and believed Jesus could help him. Jesus stopped, and rather than decide for the man, asked a simple question, "What would you like for me to do for you?" Giving dignity to Bartimeaus, He allowed Bartimeaus to tell Jesus what he wanted. Bartimeaus could have asked for something we expect a beggar to request….something like….."Jesus, give me enough money to make it through life." Make a collection for me. Make it good." He did not ask for that. He wanted something basic. He wanted to see. That is exactly what Jesus did for him. He gave sight, because Bartimeaus needed to see and wanted that gift. Jesus understood real needs and focused on meeting those needs rather than allow any crowd to dictate his actions.

We have looked at Jesus' relationships with strangers, but did he really have friends? Was He like us in normal every day kinds of relationships? I believe so. Jesus had both male and female friends who walked with Him for three years. Martha, Mary, and their brother Lazarus were friends He met in the town of Bethany just outside Jerusalem. We know two occasions when they invited Him to their home for a meal. The first recorded in Luke 10:38-40 offers insight into their relationship. These were bold women who invited Jesus the rabbi into their home. That was typically the prerogative of the men, yet they felt comfortable enough to go outside the normal bounds. The fact that Jesus accepted their offer showed His acceptance of them as well.

Martha did not abandon all the customs regarding the place of women. On one occasion, she assumed the normal role of servant preparing the meal and serving her guests. Mary, however, chose to sit with the men at Jesus' feet. She wanted to know what He was saying. She wanted to know Him. Martha took exception to her actions and scolded her in front of Jesus, but He let it be known that Mary had chosen the better thing. He was pleased to have her beside Him and share His heart with her alongside his other friends.

We see these sisters again on the occasion of the death of their brother Lazarus. During his illness, they had actually sent for Jesus thinking He would come and heal their brother. Jesus did not come in time to save Lazarus from death, but arrived four days late. When both sisters heard Jesus had arrived, they ran out to meet him. Both questioned Jesus for not coming earlier, yet He did not scold them or chide them. He seemed to understand their grief and simply told them that Lazarus would live. Both sisters trusted Him completely, though they did not understand what he was going to do. There was a depth to their relationship with Jesus that went beyond the grief of the moment. John notes Jesus wept with Martha and Mary, and that Jesus was moved in His spirit. The Jews who were there also noted how much Jesus loved Martha, Mary, and Lazarus.

I can understand these feelings having been to a number of funerals and officiating some. Every funeral is distinct. Some people in attendance are very hopeless. Others seem to work through the sadness, and are able to celebrate the life of the one who died. In every funeral, there are two kinds of people in attendance. There are those who, like the Jews, come to offer solace. They are kind and sincerely want to help. They may or may not have known the deceased, yet they are not really connected. Then you see the family and close friends who clearly participate with the family. They feel what the family feels, and love each other. Jesus displayed his deep connection with the family. It was obvious to everyone He loved these individuals. He was connected. He was not distant or fulfilling an obligation to be there.

Later that week, we observe Mary's demonstration of deep love for Jesus. Again, they had Him for dinner. Martha, as usual, was serving. Lazarus was at Jesus' feet learning and hearing His heart. John records that Mary came and poured a very costly perfume on Jesus feet and wiped it away with her hair mixed with tears. This was a very outward expression of deep love for Him. The Jews were planning on killing Him, and everyone knew He was in great danger, being in Jerusalem at this time. Mary, may have feared for his life, and chose to express herself in this way. Jesus said she was anointing Him for burial. The obvious fact is a deeply loving relationship existed between Jesus and this entire family.

Peter and the twelve apostles provide another look into the honesty of the relationships Jesus had with His friends. Each of the twelve apostles had responded to Jesus simple request to "follow" Him. He invited them into His life and to participate in His journey. They had accepted, and for three years, they walked together, sharing stories and experiences.

Each of them exchanged, what would have been described as a normal life, for a life filled with questions and uncertainty. They chose life with Jesus, because they wanted to be with Him. They shared closeness. They reclined at dinners together. At the last supper, John leaned up against Jesus to ask a question.

As we read the gospels, we see an account of very open and honest talk between friends. Jesus asked them questions every day, and had open discussions about life. They heard all His parables and asked Him what He meant. They were given the privilege of hearing detailed explanations of the deep truths He was sharing. He both praised and reprimanded them as the occasion demanded. Jesus stated Nathanial was a person without deceit. Jesus told Peter he would have great authority in the future church, yet he said to Peter on another occasion, "Get behind me Satan." He reprimanded the disciples for their selfish desire to have places of honor and praised them for their willingness to leave their old life behind to follow Him.

There was openness on Jesus part to include His friends in his work. He sent them out in pairs on two occasions to tell people in the surrounding countryside about God's plan. He had three very close friends Peter, James and John who were invited to participate in miracles such as the raising of Jairus' daughter. They were invited to the top of a mountain to see Jesus wrapped in the splendor of God and heard the Father speak directly to them. Jesus invited them to completely know His heart and share His life. He was willing to ask them to join with him in His pain. He did not try to go through life alone. His last night on earth, Jesus took these three with Him, apart from the others, and asked them to pray with Him. All three times, they went to sleep, but He kept asking. He knew Peter was going to deny Him at His greatest time of need, but Jesus never quit loving

Peter. After His resurrection, Jesus specifically told Mary to tell Peter the news. He did not want his friend to feel left out, rejected, or that He did not understand; therefore, Jesus gave specific instructions for Mary to tell Peter He was alive.

We have examined many incidences in the life of Jesus revealing the truth of His desire to know and love individual humans.

John finished his gospel with these words: *"And there are also many other things which Jesus did, which if they were written in detail, I suppose that even the world itself would not contain the books that would be written." (John 21:25)*

There is ample evidence God wants to know us and love us in the same way. He wants to have a relationship with us, and has done what it takes to make it possible. He has given us ample examples to help us get it right. He wants us to know Him, to love Him, and to have a real relationship with Him. God wants us to experience deep relationships with one another built on the foundations of being known and loved.

His invitation to us is to have a growing, deep relationship with Him along with growing, deep relationships with others. How do we do that?

DAVE COLLINS

The highest science, the loftiest speculation, the mightiest philosophy, which can ever engage our attention, is the name, the nature, the person, the work, the doings, and the existence of the great God.

C. H. Spurgeon

DAVE COLLINS

11

KNOWING & LOVING GOD

How do we find the kind of relationships we are looking for? Is it potluck? Are some people lucky, and run into the right people? Is it the luck of birth? Are some born into good families, and learn how to do it? I, personally, do not think it has anything to do with luck. Relationships are all about our choices. We go through life making choices whether we recognize it or not. We can float through life allowing our culture, our family background, or our circumstances dictate to us the kinds of choices we will make. Or, we can go back to the beginning recognizing there is a Creator who has told us, and demonstrated for us, how to live. We can go back to where we began this whole story, the place where man exchanged the truth about God for a lie. We have refused to know Him as He really is, consequently throwing all relationships out of balance. We can improve our understanding of relationships by getting to know Him.

I have to make an admission here. I like some "chick" flicks. I have even been known to "glaze" while watching some movies. I can see them over and over, and go through my glazing moments at the same time in each film. I know what's coming. I never think it's going to happen this time, but it does. The familiar scenes approach. I feel the lump in my throat. My son says we men are not allowed to cry, but we are permitted to glaze. My eyes glaze as I try to avoid eye contact with my wife. Then, I turn to her, and she is always watching me with a knowing look. My wife and I actually watch one movie together periodically, and never seem to tire of it. "You've Got Mail" is about two people who meet in a chat room on the internet, and later meet in person without knowing they chat regularly. Circumstances lead the woman to believe the man is a horrible person out to destroy her. He later discovers she is the woman with whom he has chatted, and he wants to have a deep relationship with her. His challenge is to get her to know him as he really is rather than the man she perceives him to be. In order to remove the barrier preventing her from considering the possibility of- loving him, He does what he can to help her change her mind about him.

Does that movie theme have a familiar ring to it? The relationship could not go anywhere until she knew his true character, and we cannot be in relationship with God unless we know who He really is. I'd like to go back to a passage in the Bible we have seen before, Romans 1:19-23. Paul explains there, mankind has been given enough evidence in the created order to know God. Yet, man has refused to know Him. Having been misled by our own perceptions and the things we hear, we have exchanged the truth about God for a lie. Believing the lie keeps us from knowing Him. Not knowing Him, we cannot love Him. Consequently, we turn our love to what we can see, taste and feel rather than to the One who is behind it all. Read Romans 1: 19-32 once again. Refusing to know God has impacted our relationship with everything in the world. We have become fools in the process, and in our foolishness have lost the ability on our own to have a pure relationship with God, or anybody else.

Because that which is known about God is evident within them. For since the creation of the world His invisible attributes, His eternal power and divine nature have been clearly seen, being understood through what has been made, so that they are without excuse.

For even though they knew God, they did not honor Him as

God or give thanks, but they became futile in their speculations, and their foolish heart was darkened. Professing to be wise, they became fools, and exchanged the glory of the incorruptible God for an image in the form of corruptible man and of birds and four-footed animals and crawling creatures. Therefore, God gave them over in the lusts of their hearts to impurity, so that their bodies would be dishonored among them. For they exchanged the truth of God for lie, and worshiped and served the creature rather than the Creator, who is blessed forever. Amen.
(Rom. 1:19-25)

There are physical consequences for not knowing God. Our bodies suffer. We do not know how to take care of ourselves. We over eat, and become obese. We suffer heart issues, diabetes, and a number of other physical ailments. We do not sleep well. We are anxious, and have hypertension. There is an epidemic of sexually transmitted diseases that could be wiped out completely, by following God's design. These diseases not only impact the individual infected, but those with whom the infected person has intimate contact.

Not knowing God leads to physical problems, but we are corrupt in our thinking as well. Paul calls this a depraved mind. This mindset causes us to think of ourselves first, what we want, think we deserve, or feel is our right to have. People who get in the way, become obstacles to overcome rather than fellow humans with whom we cooperate to achieve good goals for everyone. Our mind is so misguided, it can condemn the practice of all kinds of actions it calls evil while making heroes of those who practice those very evils.

I ask again, how can we overcome this situation? We can start by acknowledging the truth. We have a problem. This is not religious talk, a fanatical idea, or an exaggeration of how our world looks. We do not relate well. We envy, injure, and kill, emotionally if not physically. God has not remained aloof and distant. Instead, He came to earth out of love for mankind, and offers reconciliation. He continues to provide ways to know Him. He has done the hard part. There is, however, more we can do. We can correct the error mankind made in the first place, and truly seek to know God. If we refuse to know Him as He is, we will follow a god of our own making. Our god will become a reflection of ourselves and nothing more. Our love for God will become merely a kind of self-love.

We can know purposely seek to know to God. Spend time alone in nature, and you will discover basic truths about God. The intricate workings of nature did not happen by accident. His creativity and intellect are obvious. His order is evident in the rhythms of the days and the seasons. It is displayed in the intricate patterns of nature, and how all things fit and work together. Stare in wonder at the Milky Way, and consider the immensity of the God who put the innumerable stars in the heavens. The beauty all around us speaks volumes about the beauty of God. He is the master artist who invented color and light. Be amazed by the colors in fish, in birds, in the flowers. We live in, and are part of, the design of a Designer who is revealing Himself to anyone who will look.

There is more we can do to know God. He has taken the initiative to reveal Himself in nature, but also through the written word. The amazing testimony of God has been compiled in the Bible. It is not a book to be used as a decoration or a family keepsake. It is His letter to us. Through it, we can hear His plans for the human race, how we should respond to Him, and what He continues to do for our benefit and for His glory. Its purpose is to be read. It is meant to be studied and understood. Reading and studying God's letter to us takes time and energy, but it is crucial to knowing God. Reading the Bible helps us know ourselves, know others, and know life.

It may seem like a strange thing, but in our journey to know Him we can simply ask that He reveal Himself to us. If we are sincere, He will respond. He will speak to our conscience. After all, He made us and understands everything about our mind, emotion, and will. It may sound mystical and strange, but there is a spiritual side of humanity that hungers for the touch of God, and He is more than willing to meet us at our point of hunger to make Himself known.

We understand through experience, no relationship is instantaneous. Knowing God is a growth process. On earth, we will never know Him completely, but we can journey from this moment until our death, knowing Him better and better. Just as my relationship with my wife began with a brief encounter in a dining hall at the University, our first encounters with God are usually very simple. Over time, we know more of Him. The next step is to respond to the knowledge we currently have of Him. As we listen and grow to know God for who He is, we should find ourselves falling in love with Him. Knowing Him is the bridge of leading us to Him. Love binds us together. It comes down to a choice, beginning with a response to our conscience, the natural order, and the written word. Will we choose to know Him? Then, will we choose to love Him? Failure to respond is to follow the same path recorded in Romans. No response is a refusal to acknowledge God, and leads to the consequences listed there in the passage.

So, what is the response God is looking for? We may ask the question another way. What does God want from me, or how will God know I love Him? What do we give to someone who has everything, and needs nothing? Books have been written on this subject, but here is a simple response based on a passage in the book of Micah.

My people, what have I done to you, And how have I wearied you? Answer Me. "Indeed, I brought you up from the land of Egypt And ransomed you from the house of slavery, And I sent before you Moses, Aaron and Miriam. "My people, remember now What Balak king of Moab counseled And what Balaam son of Beor answered him, And from Shittim to Gilgal, So that you might know the righteous acts of the LORD." (Micah 6:3-5)

The people of God had begun to leave Him. They were following the old path of making up their own god rather than knowing the One who had chosen them, and revealed Himself to them. He asked them what He had done to make them grow tired of Him. He reminded them of the men He had sent to rescue them from slavery, and to show them who He was. He reminded them of their journey through the dessert, and how He had guided them, protected them and revealed himself to them through the experiences along the way. Then, the people asked a deep question, "OK God, I know you are out there. Just what is it that you want from me?" They said it this way:

With what shall I come to the LORD And bow myself before the God on high? Shall I come to Him with burnt offerings, with yearling calves? Does the LORD take delight in thousands of rams, In ten thousand rivers of oil? Shall I present my firstborn for my rebellious acts, The fruit of my body for the sin of my soul? He has told you, O man, what is good; And what does the LORD require of you But to do justice, to love kindness, And to walk humbly with your God?

Micah 6:6-8

The question is asked. God, what do you want? Do you want me to come with prescribed religious acts recorded in the Bible? Is the practice of religion the answer? Do I follow the rules, do the dos, and don't do the don'ts? Maybe that is not enough. Is there enough sacrificing I can do to satisfy God? Really, it sounds impossible. I could give all my rams. If it were possible to give enough oil to flow like a river, I would still sense God would not be satisfied. Even if I gave up the most precious thing in my life, my first-born child, would that be enough, God? Is that what it takes me to love You?

Micah gives a simple three-step answer. They are to do justice, to love mercy, and to walk humbly with God. Micah says God has told us what He wants. It is like three steps in a stairway to right living. His list begins with the top and final step. The life pleasing to God is the life that does justice. God is interested in what we do. What we do should be a reflection of what He would do. Normally, we live according to what we believe. Ultimately, we will act according to our belief system, our way of thinking. If we are racist people, we will live a life characterized by racist talk and action. If we value people, and truly want the best for our fellow man, we will live that out as well. What God wants is for people to live a life driven by justice. Doing justice is evidence that people know and love God, because God is just.

Doing justice involves actions that work for the good of others. It means owners of companies choose to give fair wages without sacrificing their own profit. One will deal honestly with his customer, give a good product, and stand behind his product. Doing justice will give a worker incentive to work hard for his wages. Doing justice means the worker gives an honest day's work for those wages knowing he or she will have every opportunity to advance and achieve according to his or her ability. Doing justice will mean one tells the truth, and does not slander his neighbor. He will not take advantage of someone who is vulnerable. Doing justice will mean providing equal opportunity to achieve to anyone willing to work hard. Doing justice will honestly evaluate how a community is doing, and work to help those in trouble. Doing justice is exemplified by the old adage that "we should do unto others as we would have others do unto us."

This is the kind of society God envisions and desires for mankind. Notice how it flies in the face of the scathing list of characteristics of those who refuse to know Him. It is not self-seeking. Neither does it ignore one's personal needs. It seeks the good of one's neighbor, and operates out of a sense of dignity and value for all. It does not excuse slothfulness or irresponsibility, and will punish and seek to amend wrongdoing. It does not play favorites or give advantage to one group over another. It does not offer excuses, but works toward resolutions of difficulties. It gives individuals responsibility in and for the community without stealing his individuality. Doing justice is good for "me", and it is good for "us."

As I write these words, I recognize how far we fall short of doing justice. Our world falls short, because we cannot do justice until we have taken the step below it. We are to love mercy. Loving mercy is an attitude of the heart. It is the heart that empowers one to sacrifice money, time, and effort to help someone in need. Mercy is driven by love. Remember, love looks at another, seeing their need, and responds to that need. Loving mercy is doing love. Doing mercy can be translated "loving-kindness". It is one of the terms used to describe the character of God. Again, we see

God wants us to become like Himself. His desire is for our character to change to one that is not self-centered. Our heart should be inclined to look for ways to love others. It is a heart predisposed to love. Loving hearts builds character. With this kind of heart, one will naturally do justice. It will be the natural flow. Again, we reflect the character of God who acts justly motivated by and flowing out of His love.

The heart is a funny thing. I find it a fickle thing. There have been times when I have seen the proper course of action, and chosen to change. After much effort, after some successes and some failures, I have been able to change a habit. For example, when I was in junior high school, I wanted to fit in. The guys I knew who were popular and powerful cursed a lot, so I took up their language. The day came when my language was laced with curse words without my even thinking. It had become the way I spoke, and part of my heart. One day I noticed something that changed everything. I began listening to the words of my friends, and others around school. I observed the very poorest students were the most adept at cursing. They did not seem to know any adjectives or have the capacity to articulate a thought. Adjectives were replaced by a curse word or a series of curse words. I realized I was limiting myself with the same habit. I chose to change. I began to eliminate all cursing from my vocabulary replacing that kind of talk with words having specific meaning. My behavior did change, but there is one observation of note. My motivation to change was purely selfish. I did not want to appear to be stupid. I changed to a certain extent, but my heart was the same. People saw a more sophisticated person, but my heart was still centered on what I wanted for myself.

There have been times, after seeing the evil I am capable of doing through my self-driven heart, that I wanted to change. I have gone through the same kind of process to change by using observation, evaluation, and choosing an action plan. I thought I could change my heart with the same tools that helped me change a habit. I have seen very different results. I have known the proper action to take, buckled down, and sworn I would begin doing the right. I wanted to do it. I wanted to succeed. Yet, I found myself repeating old actions over and over. The very thing I wanted to do, I could not do. My heart, at its core, is a very stubborn thing, and it would not change. I could not subdue it or change it in my own strength.

Micah says, we can never do justice or love mercy without taking the first step. Step one makes all the others possible. It begins when we choose to walk humbly with God. Walking is the key. Walking with God is how we get to know God, and love will flow out of knowing Him.

Remember the story of blind Bartimeaus? He called out to Jesus to have mercy on him. Like Bartimeaus, we begin life blind to God and unable to see how life should work. A changed heart, like changed vision, begins with what we know. We must, like Bartimeaus, know that Jesus is able to fix our heart problem. We must act on what we know. Bartimeaus trusted Jesus enough to ask for help, regained his sight, and began following Jesus. He literally began walking down the road with Jesus. He listened to what Jesus said. He observed what Jesus did. He began a journey with God, walking with Jesus. He began a whole new set of experiences in life where God was involved. Bartimeaus did not choose his destination. He was not in control. He followed Jesus.

That is what walking with God is like for us. It may not appear to be physically walking beside a man we can touch and hear, but in some ways, it is the same. We walk with Jesus in our hearts and in our souls as we invite Him to be with us in our everyday lives. He is there when we pray or ponder the words He has given us in the Bible. He is there when we begin to make choices based on our understanding of His character, His desire. We follow, as we sense He is pointing us in a new direction. On the journey, we will see Him act and faithfully, do what He has promised, prompting us to trust Him at deeper levels. We will want to know what God thinks and who He is at the core of His being. We will find ourselves giving Him access to our deepest needs and desires, learning to listen to His counsel on all matters of life. In the process, we move from knowing about God to truly knowing Him, to loving Him, to strive to become more and more like Him.

We join Him on a journey that will take us to places we will not imagine. It is a lifelong adventure, involving a process in which our hearts completely change over time. Our desires change. Our motives change. Our character changes. The things I cannot make my heart do become natural as I follow Jesus. As I walk with Him and know Him deeply, my heart is drawn to Him.

There is a caveat to walking with God, though, and it is key to the process. We must walk humbly with Him. Humble is a hard word to grasp. It sounds like I must make myself a doormat. Does it mean I become someone who gets the dirt and grime wiped off the shoes of the One I follow? I prefer to envision humility as power under control. I saw power under control when my daughter rode horses. I was amazed watching her perform in the ring doing dressage with those powerful animals. She had them prance, or walk with a graceful swing of their legs. They could go forward, backward, or diagonally across the ring. Amazingly, she never seemed to move. She remained straight in the saddle barely moving, in symphony with the gate of the horse. I witnessed grace and power in motion, yet seemingly without any effort at all. She told me how she did it. She simply applied slight pressure with her knees, or used her pinky finger on the reigns to increase or decrease pressure on the bit. Her horse was so sensitive to her light pressure that he was able to "hear" her commands and respond to them. These horses were no doormats. They were very powerful, yet they were willing to submit to my daughter's commands. They were very "humble."

I do not believe God wants to beat us or yell at us to get our attention. He wants us to be attentive to Him, sensitive to His commands, and willing to respond to the lightest touch or pressure from Him. As we humbly walk with Him, the journey becomes a powerful force in our lives. Talk with Him about whatever you encounter on the journey. Share your heart with Him, and listen to what you hear from Him. This is what prayer is all about. On the journey, we will experience God in ways those who are not walking with Him cannot understand. We will begin to know Him at a very deep level. As we see Him work in our lives and see the goodness of His heart, we will begin to change in our own hearts. As we see Him hard situations and turn them to good. We will know Him at a deeper level. As He gives us power to act in ways we could not act before, we will know Him experientially. We will begin to do things differently. We will do justice, because we have a heart predisposed to mercy and kindness. We will know God intimately, and we will love Him deeply.

Jesus said it Himself when he was with His disciples. Having just finished the last meal they would have together, Jesus told them what their future relationship would be like. This is what He said:

He who has my commands and keeps them is the one who loves me; and he who loves Me will be loved by My Father, and I will love him and will disclose Myself to him. (John 14:21)

Jesus described what the relationship journey is like with Him. The journey involves knowing his commands. They are found in the Scriptures for us today, and we can choose to listen or not. As we begin to hear God's word to us, we must make a choice. Will we do what He is asking? God in the person of The Holy Spirit will apply slight pressure in our conscience to do what we understand God The Father is telling us to do. When we submit by saying yes, we are loving God. He loves that response. Jesus says He will reveal more of Himself to us every time we say yes to His direction.

We began this chapter with two questions. How do I know God, and how do I love God? Micah has shown us the process. Begin with the little things we know about God. Respond to Him as we hear Him speak. Learn more of Him every time we trust Him and submit to His direction. That is the journey. That is how we walk with God. That is what it takes to know Him. That is how we love Him.

Incredibly, this walk will change everything about us. Walking humbly with God will lead our heart to love mercy. Loving hearts will direct us to do justice. Our whole way of living life, especially relationships, will change.

DAVE COLLINS

The body is a house of many windows: there we all sit, showing ourselves and crying on the passers-by to come and love us.

Robert Louis Stevenson

DAVE COLLINS

12

KNOWING & LOVING MYSELF

After talking in the last chapter about changing one's heart to think outside itself, it may seem odd to talk about loving ourselves. This is a book about relationships. The bottom line is our relationship with God, but we must expand from that point. The next link to having whole and complete relationships with others is to understand whom we are and properly love ourselves. The problem is not that we do not love ourselves, but that we love ourselves in the wrong way. Focusing on ourselves prevents us from expending ourselves in the effort to know and love others.

One day a religious leader asked Jesus, "What is the greatest commandment. Jesus' response was this,

"You shall love the Lord your God with all your heart, and with all your soul, and with all your mind. This is the great and foremost commandment. The second is like it, you shall love your neighbor as yourself. (Matt. 22:37)

Loving God is truly the starting place, but Jesus quickly put a second command behind the first. His heart, so in tune with our relational needs, commands us to love people around us. The interesting thing is He says we are to love them as we love ourselves.

Some suggest Jesus is teaching us to love ourselves first, which will enable us to love others. They equate low self-esteem with lack of love for ourselves. We hear talk of people who hate themselves. We hear people say, "I hate my looks", or "I wish I wasn't so dumb", or "If I could only….." Can such thinking be, in reality, an indication of how we evaluate our self rather than whether we love our self?

My contention is, we all love ourselves. We may not appreciate who we are, and we may be envious of others wishing for their physical characteristics or mental capabilities. We may loathe a habit or a path in life we have chosen. but at the core of our being, we love our self. We cannot quit thinking of ourselves. We are the first subjects of our thoughts. We dwell on things we wish for, things we wish to accomplish, accolades we wish to receive, our past, our future, our fears, our pleasures. We cannot stop thinking about ourselves. When we are hungry, we will drop everything to eat. We make sure we are clothed properly. We are obsessed with being warm enough or cool enough. We will skip important tasks or activities just to get a little extra sleep. If we find pleasure in something, we will sacrifice what we actually need in order to experience the pleasure. Is there honestly any question that every one of us loves himself?

Jesus is teaching, we are to love others just as much as we already love ourselves. We should be concerned about their desires, their fears, their dreams, their needs as much as we are our own. Wow, Jesus is asking a lot! The problem for us is we have such intense love for ourselves; it becomes difficult to love others with equal intensity. Sometimes, we are incorrect in assessing our real need, or we look to the wrong places to get those needs met. It is as if we focus on a beautiful mountain peak, thinking on its summit exists the most beautiful place in the world. We set out on an arduous climb, obsessed with getting to that incredible place, convinced the mountain top riches will be worth whatever it costs to get there. However, upon reaching the top, we find thistles and rocks. We look to the side and notice a lower peak covered with flowers, trees, and all sorts of beautiful things. We climbed the wrong mountain.

The reason our relationship with others does not work or leaves us wounded is we are seeking something from them they cannot provide. We have misunderstood what we need and where to get it. We cannot know and love others purely until we come to grips with who we really are, and what we really need. Having lost sight of our God-given design, we tend to use people rather than love them. We allow them to know us only up to a point, and we find the commitment to know them is too difficult.

Again, Jesus provides an example for us to understand what we must know about ourselves. At the last meal He had with his disciples, Jesus talked about what He knew about Himself. He began the evening in a surprising way. Even though He was their teacher and leader, and they saw Him as their master. Jesus did a humble talk of a lowly servant. He washed everyone's feet. John describes the scene this way.

Now before the feast of the Passover, Jesus knowing that his hour had come and that He would depart out of this world to the Father, having loved his own who were in the world, He loved them to the end. During supper, the devil having already put into the heart of Judas Iscariot, the son of Simon, to betray Him, Jesus, knowing that the Father had given all things into His hands, and that He had come forth from God and was going back to God, got up from supper, and laid aside His garments, and taking a towel, He girded Himself. Then He poured water into a basin, and began to wash the disciples' feet and to wipe them with the towel with which He was girded. (John 13:1-5)

Jesus knew what He was about to face, the suffering, the humiliation, and the abandonment. He knew his hour had come. He knew Judas was about to betray Him. He could have done what I would have done, and focused on His own problems and pain. Yet, He chose to meet the needs of his friends. He gave himself to them going out of His way to love them by taking the role of a servant, even washing their feet. He could do that, because He knew Himself and had a proper understanding of self-love. Jesus knew He had come from the Father. He knew His past, where He came from, who He was, and why He was sent. Understanding the significance and value of having been prepared, and sent by the Father, He applied what the past meant to His present. Knowing His past prepared Him to live confidently and purposefully in the present. His present was significant. All things had been given into His hands. He had everything He needed to act as He was called to do. He also knew His future. He was going back to the Father. There was no need for fear or doubt about the unknown. No present circumstance would change His future. Even death could not take away what was surely being held for Him. There was nothing to keep Him from acting in the present as He was called to act. Everything Jesus knew about His past, present, and future empowered Him to make choices every moment of His life. He chose to live life based on the reality of His life, refusing to give in to the pressures of the world, or seek immediate gratification, or self-comfort. Self-love for Jesus did not mean feeling good in the moment. It was about understanding His identity, value, and purpose in life.

We have the same opportunity to know our past, present and future. This knowledge about ourselves is very powerful in providing the strength we need to make very tough choices in life. Properly understanding of our self provides the ability to choose between false self-love and perceptions of where our needs appear to be met, versus knowing the truth about our self, and where our needs will truly be met. The false love is grounded in what the bible calls the lust of the flesh, the lust of the eyes, and the pride of life. It is the same lie Eve, and later Adam chose to follow, and it led to mankind's downfall. True self-love though, is grounded in the reality of who God created us to be, and how He has equipped us for life. It recognizes the truth of God's promises, and is willing to follow God's direction, knowing God will meet all our needs.

Proper self-love, and the ability to make proper choices, come as we learn from our physical past and understand our spiritual past. We must know our purpose. We must also know the reality of our future rather than guess the future or try to manipulate the future. How does this work?

Everyone's life consists of two pasts. One past has been lived from birth to the present. It is the accumulation of moments lived each day on earth. It includes the mundane nature of life like eating, sleeping, working, and relating with people around us. Part of our past include special moments of great impact. Some were devastating and difficult, while others lift us to the heights. Each moment contributes to who we become and the legacy we leave behind in life. Those moments slipped by as days and years eventually becoming memories. These experiences contribute both positively and negatively toward the development of our character, our understanding of whom we are, and our perception of where to find joy and fulfillment in life. Every one of us knows all or part of his past. It is very powerful, and has the capacity to control each of us in the present and the future. Our past can be a barrier or a positive influence toward a proper self-love.

Our Physical Past

Our physical past has a way of training us, and growing us up. It can be a very good thing. When we are very small, our parents tell us not to touch. "It's hot," they say. One day we touch a hot object learning what "hot" means. We learn hot is a dangerous thing when it is not given proper respect. We learn from past mistakes, and their consequences. A family helps build into its children moral values and beliefs, as parents impose consequences for immoral acts done by their children. Consequences imposed by one's culture further helps influence a person's values. Unfortunately, parents and culture teach both truth and evil through its influence. Our response to what we see and what we are taught leads to good or evil in our personal character. I only need mention racism as an example. It is generally passed on through the influence of family and culture.

One friend told me about her family. My father was a member of the KKK most of his life. My grandfather, though very wealthy, was a Grand Dragon in Arkansas. I grew up with extreme prejudice around me, only to reject those beliefs and attitudes choosing to go the opposite direction.

There are many positive and negative aspects to our past. Growing up in a family with drug-addicted parents who are confusing and behave inconsistently is a problem. Their child does not receive dependable tools for making decisions or understanding how to make choices. There is inconsistent training regarding moral choices, and how to relate to others. One can grow up in a family where tragedy strikes. A parent dies unexpectedly or divorce happens. A child growing up in such a family can assign a false meaning to the tragic event. They can grow up thinking bad things are their fault, because they are bad people. That false belief from the past has the power to control the decisions one makes for an entire life. Life builds one event stacked on another, and we tend to place some meaning or significance to each event. Many times, we are able to understand the circumstances or someone can explain what has happened. However, many times, especially as children, we are left to assign our own childish interpretation or meaning to the events that have transpired. As a child, we can place devastatingly harmful meanings to events we do not understand. As experiences accumulate with the corresponding meanings we have attached, we develop a paradigm or lens through which we see life. These lenses, built by our families and the world around us, are often false. Moreover, the false thinking, very deeply rooted in our souls, is hard to dislodge or ignore. Our false thinking serves as the center of our decision-making, our emotions, and it impacts how we live life, especially regarding relationships.

We do not like to talk about it, but another enemy is at work in our life, using circumstances and opportunities life presents to create a false understanding of what life is meant to be. He is the same enemy faced Eve in the garden, and Jesus faced in the desert, and he employs the same arguments with us he presented to them. He is constantly presenting us with lies sounding so good or right, they are hard not to believe. These lies enter our thoughts providing the opportunity and the temptation to live for self-gratification, personal comfort, and power. These thoughts run along the lines of "If only I had....... I would be happy. It's their fault I don't have what I need..... I have to lie about this... Besides it's only a small lie." Small thoughts can be acted on once, but they are usually repeated and become a habit. A habit becomes a way of life, which becomes our legacy. Many of us live our lives based on lies of various kinds. These lies lead to the brokenness I described earlier where things become more important than people, or people are viewed as a means to meet my own needs.

I have told you part of my physical past that impacted my sense of self. My family provided the greatest source of information about who I am, and what I should be like. My earliest memory, I have already shared, occurred when I was less than 5 years old. Suffering through pneumonia during the Christmas season, I was too sick to participate, but I remember being stuffed into a large chair with a big quilt. I remember the sense of care and comfort my family provided. I knew I was loved. There is still a place in my mind wanting to feel that same sense of love and comfort. I have looked for those feelings in many ways, in many people, and in many circumstances, but it is a hunger that is never satisfied completely on earth.

I have shared some negative experiences leading to false thinking. I learned early on in my family if one were going to do something, it had to be done right. There was no room for error. I was always fearful of getting things wrong. I wondered if I could ever measure up. You have read the story of my music class in the third grade compounding self-doubts and creating in me a resolve to avoid being visible. There was another episode in the 9th grade that confirmed my fears. I was promoted to an accelerated English class from the normal English class curriculum. At the beginning of the year, everyone in class was to write a paragraph about some subject I don't remember now. Later, the teacher chose two of us to write our paragraphs on the blackboard. There was a moment of high spirits when my name was called. I remember thinking, maybe this is what I can do. I am being recognized. At the blackboard, I peeked over at the girl writing next to me. Her handwriting was beautiful. I could not help comparing her flowing letters to my scrawling, but I finished my work and sat down satisfied. Then it happened. The teacher went to my work and began drawing circles around what seemed like every other word. They were misspelled or incorrectly used. I was mortified.

She had chosen the best paragraph, and compared it to the worst. I felt like a loser and wanted to hide. I did hide. My wounded self-love led me to go inside myself, quietly seeking invisibility even more intensely.

There were some wonderful things about my childhood. Athletics had a profound influence on my thinking and development. They provided a sense of purpose, and a place I could accomplish something. Athletics only lasted until college for me. I was too small, and not skilled enough to play beyond high school. It is not surprising after I entered college seeking to become an optometrist that I later changed to the one thing I felt I could do. I ended up majoring in physical education intent on coaching. I lived life in search of comfort and love, wondering how anyone could love me. I believed in working hard and doing things well. Yet, I was always fearful my work would not measure up. I sat through many meetings full of ideas, but too fearful to express them. I always set limits to how much I would reveal of myself for fear others would see my weakness. I found it hard to accept praise fearing it would immediately be turned into horror as exemplified by my experience in English class. My present was controlled by my physical past. I had a very skewed idea about life, and where I fit in. Consequently, as a quiet unseen person, I was considered a nice guy, but relationships were pretty shallow and manipulated by me. Lack of understanding about my true significance led to a constant inner battle seeking recognition and love while pushing people away. Fear they might discover the truth about me controlled my life.

Our Spiritual Past

There is another past, unseen, and spiritual. This past is not muddied by the falsehood. It is the reality of our existence, and holds the truth about life. It existed before we were born. God has not been silent about our past and what He thinks about us. The Psalms speak to the reality of our spiritual past.

O LORD, You have searched me and known me. You know when I sit down and when I rise up; You understand my thought from afar. You scrutinize my path and my lying down, And are intimately acquainted with all my ways. Even before there is a word on my tongue, Behold, O LORD, You know it all. You have enclosed me behind and before, And laid Your hand upon me.

For You formed my inward parts You wove me in my mother's womb. I will give thanks to You, for I am fearfully and wonderfully made; Wonderful are Your works, And my soul knows it very well. My frame was not hidden from You, When I was made in secret, And skillfully wrought in the depths of the earth; Your eyes have seen my unformed substance; And in Your book were all written The days that were ordained for me, When as yet there was not one of them. Psalm 139: 1-5; 13-16.

I love this passage of scripture. It tells the truth about us. It reveals how God knows me in and out. He knows what I am doing every day. He knows what I am thinking. He knows what I am saying. He knows me intimately. I like to think of God seeing me at my best. It feels like He is at my game cheering for me. However, I must remember this passage says God knows every action, every thought. All my worst thoughts and actions are equally in plain view to God. Knowing me this way, He still lays his hand on me. I picture this as a dad tussling his son's hair. It is an affectionate touch. It is the touch of a dad blessing his son. What's more, I understand God made me. He wove me together. I picture an artist putting together his best work. God has thought about my design. He knew what He wanted to see, and skillfully put me together. It is true I am fearfully and wonderfully made. He has put something of His own beauty within me, because in Genesis God says He made each of us in His own image and in His likeness. Who I am and how I live somehow reflects what God is like. His own beauty and wonder is woven into who I am. What does God think of his workmanship? Not only does He like what He has made, He loves you and me extravagantly. He delights in us, and delights in being around us. This all began before each of us was born.

Here then, is the reality of our individual existence. In God's eyes, we are beautiful. We have incredible value. He likes us. He loves us. He planned you and me before we were born. He is blessing us this moment. We will see shortly that He has given gifts to help His children lead purposeful, bountiful, lives. Understanding this reality prompted me to ask myself the questions, "why do I doubt my value, my worth, my ability in life, and why should I believe anything that would cast me as ugly or worthless?" I was prompted to question the kind of life I was choosing to live. If it was true I was built in God's image, shouldn't I be living that way? Was I allowing faulty thinking from my physical past to cloud the reality of my present, robbing me of the kind of life I was built to live? There came a point in my physical life, where I realized the way I was living did not make any sense. I was living with only one grid from which to make decisions….the physical past was dictating how I was making choices. That all changed in my early twenties. The moment I heard about Jesus and trusted Him and the work He did to give me life, my spiritual past intersected with my physical past. My corrupted mind, that previously did not know God or His truth, began to think clearly based on truth rather than on how I had interpreted life growing up. There was a new me. I began a journey learning the truth about who I am. I began to believe the things God said about me, and reject what I had believed previously. In mentally returning to my past, I began to reinterpret everything. I had to look at those events through a new lens to gain a proper understanding of those events. I had to learn how my interpretation of life experiences was impacting my present decision-making.

Thus began a journey of culling errors, and learning truth. I have learned my parents loved me, but they had a problem with expectations. I had some poor teachers. I truly cannot sing a note, but inability to sing does not make me a bad person, an unacceptable person, or even a flawed person. Life is not about athletics or competition. Relationships are complicated. They are crucial to life, but they are not about me. I am still learning to discern which things matter, but I have a different source for understanding. I know my journey of discovery will be a lifelong process.

I am remembering the good lessons from my physical past, lessons I need to cling to. I understand some of the things that influenced me, and molded me to be who I truly am. I do not need to deviate from reality. You will not see me audition for any musical. However, I do not need to fear my inability to sing. God has a sense of humor. I was on Young Life staff for 29 years, and once a week during "club," I sang with high school kids. I learned how to play guitar, and actually "led" singing a few times. Those clubs were disasters, so I learned to look for others talented to do what I could not do and I let them use their talents. I tried to find others who could sing to fill the void I could never fill. I love music, and how it speaks directly to my soul. Knowing myself, I understand the creative bent that draws me to things like music and the arts, and I follow my passion to develop artistic skills. I was not a good writer in the 9th grade, but I have worked at the craft. How ironic that I am writing a book after being used as the example of the worst writer in class! The fact you are reading this book is testament to the fact we can overcome obstacles like limited abilities, fear, and emotional pain. We can be strong, productive, and joyful people regardless of our background.

God has intertwined my physical past with my spiritual past, to help me be true to my purpose. It has been a difficult yet rewarding journey. Though feeling awkward and out of place often, I have never known such comfort and peace. I know I have purpose. I know who I am, and need not fear what others say about me. I know my value. I know I am loved. I believe I am known completely, because my Maker designed me. He made me well. My task is to live well according to His design. I do love myself, but I do not make choices as I did before. I seek to make the right choice based on the reality of who I am, and what God has in mind rather than out of a sense of fear, self-protection, or manipulation of people.

There was a crucial life changing moment. We must acknowledge God's existence, seek to know Him, and build a loving relationship with Him. Until my physical past was joined to my spiritual past, I made choices based on the only thing I knew, my physical experience. We cannot know anything about our spiritual life until we are given that life. Consequently, Jesus talks about being born again. New life comes when we trust Christ's death and resurrection as payment for all the wrong we have chosen in life. Until that birth, I only had one way to see life. It was based on what I could interpret from my physical life, the things I observed in the lives of those who had lived beside me, on my culture's teaching, and on the written words of those who lived before me. All these things were filtered through a flawed, foolish, mind. With such a limited physical perspective of life, I missed all the beauty I was created to see. My choices were skewed, as I tried to meet my unmet needs. I needed understanding from both perspectives to have freedom in relationships. I never allowed others to know me deeply, because of fear. People knew about me, but not in depth. That same fear prevented me from knowing others deeply. I did not understand what love was all about, and did the best I could to be liked. I could not dislodge the fears and false thinking until I understood where they came from, and what was actually true. I needed the spiritual dimension of my past to put it all together. Once I began understanding my past, especially the spiritual impact, my self-love changed, allowing me to change the way I lived my present.

Our Present

I was watching a golf tournament when the announcer said the leader of the tournament needed to stay in the present. That is a profound statement. A golfer who dwells on a previous poor shot pretty much ensures he will continue to make poor shots. He is unable to focus on the now, what he must do in the present moment. The execution of the present shot is the most important thing about his game. His former shots all contributed to the current position, but they are gone. All he has is the current shot, which will make its own contribution. Furthermore, if he begins to think about challenges on the holes ahead, he will not function well on his current hole, increasing chances he will do poorly on future holes.

Now is where we live, even though now is constantly changing. If we live in the past, we will be out of step with the present. The past is gone. New things have come. We may have fond memories, and wish to relive them, but that can only happen in our memory. We will never recreate those moments, and risk wasting our present trying. Neither can we dwell on the pain of the past, or keep going back wondering if we can fix it or get rid of it. The past will always be there, and it has the power to rob us of the present if we let it. We must learn from it, then leave it. The future is not the place to dwell either. Wishing for better days, will not help our present days. That is not to say we should not plan and prepare for the future. We can use our present wisely, preparing for the future, but we must never forget no guarantees exist for our tomorrows on earth.

The problem is we do not adequately understand present reality. It is confused unless it is understood from a spiritual perspective. Our development took place in this world, in physical life, and through numerous teachers who gave us both good and bad information. Our interpretation of that information influences our worldview. In the culture of the United States, we have primarily been taught there are unlimited supplies in the world. Working hard, planning, and going after what we want, is what it takes to get the prize. What we possess is very important to us. How we look is very important. Status and influence are highly prized. We strive for these things thinking they will bring fulfillment and satisfaction in life. Our present can be consumed with the pursuit of these kinds of things, at the expense of important life issues and relationships.

Our culture teaches that happiness is the ultimate goal in life. We say we only want to be happy, or we want our kids to be happy, thinking it is found in various pursuits. Yet, happiness is very illusive. Obstacles to our pursuits rob us of happiness. Circumstances become difficult. Life is hard. Not everyone is able to achieve all they want. We may achieve all the things we think bring life only to experience a haunting and uncomfortable emptiness. Consider all that has been written about the mid-life crises. Men have scratched and clawed their way to the top of the mountain of happiness, and found emptiness. They have climbed and worked obsessively to reach the top discovering their ladder leaned against the wrong mountain. They may have everything they thought would bring happiness, yet find themselves lonely. They may have a family, but no connection to their children or wife. They may be a family only in the sense of living in the same house. Even worse, they may have started a family and destroyed it through infidelity or divorce in their pursuit of happiness.

Many of us have discovered our present includes work, achievement, adventure and fun times, but these are not the goals that count most. We were designed for more. Remember, God designed us. He formed our inward parts, and nobody makes anything without having a purpose in mind. As a painter, I think about each work I begin. What is it I want to say through this piece? How can light and color be employed to accomplish my goal? What will enhance the design or help the viewer's eye see what I want them to see? We can illustrate this concept with a computer. It began as a thought. Its inventors had a purpose in mind, hoping to increase productivity and achievement for more people. The design of a computer is not for the purpose of serving as a paperweight, or a doorstop, even though it is capable of serving those functions. Even so, our life has a grander purpose than making a living, having fun, or having power and influence. Our Designer and Creator has much to say about this.

The reality of our present purpose is a spiritual reality intertwined with our physical lives.

Then God said, "Let Us make man in Our image, according to Our likeness; and let them rule over the fish of the sea and over the birds of the sky and over the cattle and over all the earth, and over every creeping thing that creeps on the earth." God created man in His own image, in the image of

God He created him; male and female He created them. God blessed them; and God said to them, "Be fruitful and multiply, and fill the earth, and subdue it; and rule over the fish of the sea and over the birds of the sky and over every living thing that moves on the earth." Gen. 1:26-28

Somehow, we look like God. We are to act like Him. God has designed us to be much like a mirror. Seeing us, God wants to see the reflection of His character, His goodness, His love. We are reflectors. Our present purpose is to reflect what God is like as we go through life. That pleases Him. We will find our greatest joy in life by reflecting God well, and we will find fulfillment living according to our design.

God created us to rule over His creation. Consequently, we are created for work. Our physical world is important to God; therefore, how we manage our days on earth is significant to Him. It is not about us, but about reflecting His character as we manage the work He has given us to accomplish. We are created to live as families by being fruitful and multiplying. Relationships, beginning with our family, are central to God's purpose for us. We cannot work to the detriment of those relationships. Our purpose is best lived in the balance of work and relationships. We get into difficulty when we allow a false worldview to alter our present purpose. Living outside our God given purpose causes us to lean our ladders against the wrong mountain. "Climbing the wrong mountain," fulfillment will be illusive, and joy will disappear in the search for fickle happiness.

God has given us specific information regarding our present purpose beyond the idea of working and relating.

For we are His workmanship, created in Christ Jesus for good works, which God prepared beforehand so that we would walk in them. Eph. 2:10

And He gave some as apostles, and some as prophets, and some as evangelists, and some as pastors and teachers, for the equipping of the saints for the work of service, to the building up of the body of Christ; until we all attain to the unity of the faith, and of the knowledge of the Son of God, to a mature man, to the measure of the stature which belongs to the fullness of Christ. Eph. 4:11-13

With our physical life in mind, God designed us and knit us together in our mother's womb. He designed us to do good works. He thought of us in the spiritual past with a design and purpose in mind. He gave us talents and skills. Then, He gave us physical present experiences to teach and equip us to accomplish the works He had in mind.

For example, I was a football coach. When the boys came out for the team, I made a visual assessment of each boy. I noted the larger guys, because I knew my line had to block effectively. The smallest players on a football team never play tackle. There is a reason. They would be killed, and so would the running backs. If I am smart enough to design a football team around the physical attributes of my players, God is certainly able to equip me for the work He has prepared for me. Part of what happens as we grow up in our physical world is the development of skills and talents needed to accomplish the work God wants us to do. Our life experiences are very significant. They are not wasted. Even my experiences in the third grade and the ninth grade, helped prepare me for the job I was given to do as a Young Life leader. I had a heightened awareness of the pain some kids face regularly. I was able to understand, and connect with some kids who lived with great emotional pain. I was able to help them discover their value and beauty. I was built to know them, and to love them.

Not only do we have built in skills and talents, but God gives us a bonus. When we trust Christ and enter God's family, He gives us a bonus, spiritual gifts. They vary with every person. God chooses what He will give according to His purpose and design for us. Spiritual gifts help us reflect God's character. They are helpful in relating to others. His gifts also equip us to help one another be better reflectors of His character. We are designed to be in relationship with others who are walking with Christ. We all have the job of helping one another grow in maturity. Part of our purpose is to influence each other to be better reflectors. It is a present reality of our lives no matter our circumstance or place in life. It is further reminder that life is not centered in us. We do not love ourselves by selfishly placing our ladder against the mountain of self-gratification. We are to know and love others in a deep relationship. Relationships will affect our choices as we live the life God has built us, and designed us to live. We never have to wonder about our value or purpose. Living according to this design will produce the greatest joy in life.

The Future

There is one more thing to think about in considering how to love ourselves well. It is our future. As I said before, we can worry about our future, or waste effort trying to control it. Another option is to believe with certainty what God has revealed about our future.

Knowledge of the future can strengthen us in the present. Consider this promise from God.

Therefore, my beloved brethren, be steadfast, immovable, always abounding in the work of the Lord, knowing that your toil is not in vain in the Lord. 1 Cor. 15:58

He says how we live our present is not useless. It all has a purpose. Every moment of our life has value. We are encouraged to keep going no matter how bleak the future looks. Our present work is not in vain. For example, as a football player and a coach, I have experienced "millions" of wind sprints. As a player, I hated that time at the end of practice. We would line up by units, sprint 40 yards, turn around, and repeat the process, as I said, what seemed like millions of times. We thought the coaches were trying to kill us. I looked at their faces and observed a strange kind of grin. It was like they were really enjoying torturing us. The grin was not about torture. It was a knowing grin. They had done their own millions of wind sprints. They had a favorite line, "you'll thank me for these wind sprints in the fourth quarter of the game this weekend." As a coach, I wore the same grin, because it is true. Those wind sprints hardened us, preparing us for the most difficult part of the game ahead. They were not in vain!

Another aspect of this promise can be illustrated by life insurance. When I was 27, I began contributing to a pension. It was a small amount. I thought little about it the first few months it came out of my paycheck. Eventually, I almost forgot about it. My focus was on the present, what I got each month. In my 60's now, things have changed for me. I am so appreciative of the future thinking leadership that had us save a little each month to prepare for the future. We cannot control the future, but every one of us has one. As we near the end of life, what we did in the past helps us rest in our current present. Even in this example, we must understand reality. Retirement is still future and out of my control. The economy could fail. Catastrophes happen. Past preparations will probably serve well in my future, but ultimately, true rest comes by trusting God. In all times and all circumstances, peace is found in reliance on God. He does control the future, and He does offer security. God has told us some sure bets in our future. These promises are part of our hope. Our physical present will come to an end one day. The sure hope of our future provides confidence to face whatever comes our way in the present. We gain courage to know and love regardless of present circumstances. Look at these wonderful promises.

Do not let your heart be troubled; believe in God, believe also in Me. In My Father's house are many dwelling places; if it were not so, I would have told you for I go to prepare a place for you. If I go and prepare a place for you, I will come again and receive you to Myself, that where I am, there you may be also. John 14:1-3

The first promise in our future is that Jesus is preparing a place for us in Heaven. This is not wishful thinking or silly hope. It is His promise to us. Life on earth is uncertain, and often difficult. There is a promise that its end is not the end. He will be there with us, and our joy will be complete. We can rely on His promise.

For no man can lay a foundation other than the one which is laid, which is Jesus Christ. Now if any man builds on the foundation with gold, silver, precious stones, wood, hay, straw, each man's work will become evident; for the day will show it because it is to be revealed with fire, and the fire itself will test the quality of each man's work. If any man's work which he has built on it remains, he will receive a reward. If any man's work is burned up, he will suffer loss; but he himself will be saved, yet so as through fire. 1 Cor. 3:11-15

This is my wind sprint promise. It reminds me how much I loved winning football games. I loved it when in the fourth quarter, I was still strong, and my opponent was wheezing.

The winning made the work worth it. I cannot imagine what my future rewards will be in Heaven, but I am sure they will be incomparably better than a "W" in the win column. When life is hard, and I struggle to catch my breath, I think about this promise. It keeps me going. Furthermore, the rewards are based on the gifts God has given me. He designed me, and asks me to do things I am capable of doing. I do not have to compare myself to the apostle Paul or anyone else to feel good about myself. Some may get more rewards, and some may get less, but I am trusting He will give the perfect reward for each of us. We can be encouraged knowing if we fail at something Jesus wants us to do, He does not kick us off the team. We forfeit a reward we could have had, but we still get to be with Him. We can rest in that thought if we fail to do our best.

We have an eternity pension. We put a little away each day for our eternity. Jesus promised He will reward us for faithfulness. Trust Him. I could have refused to put anything in my pension account, and spent it all in the 29 years I worked in Young Life, but my later years will be better off having invested and earned interest. I am counting on a rich eternity based on God's promise.

For it is just like a man about to go on a journey, who called his own servants and entrusted his possessions to them. To one he gave five talents, to another, two, and to another, one, each according to his own ability; and he went on his journey. Immediately the one who had received the five talents went and traded with them, and gained five more talents. In the same manner, the one who had received the two talents gained two more. But he who received the one talent went away, and dug a hole in the ground and hid his master's money.

"Now after a long time the master of those servants came

and settled accounts with them. The one who had received the five talents came up and brought five more talents, saying, 'Master, you entrusted five talents to me. See, I have gained five more talents.' His master said to him, 'Well done, good and faithful servant. You were faithful with a few things, I will put you in charge of many things enter into the joy of your master.'

"Also the one who had received the two talents came up and said, 'Master, you entrusted two talents to me. See, I have gained two more talents.' His master said to him, 'Well done, good and faithful servant. You were faithful with a few things, I will put you in charge of many things enter into the joy of your master.' Matt. 25:14-23

This parable reminds me of my youth when I would do incredible things to hear praise from one of my coaches. There was something about my sense of honor and value that got a shot in the arm from words of praise or affirmation. I know much of the emotion was misplaced, but I gained a valuable lesson. I am now imagining what it will feel like to hear "well done" from the One who can legitimately give that honor. We strive all our lives to please our fathers on earth. How much more will it mean to hear praise from the Father of all fathers? This desire to hear praise from God can especially move us to be who we are designed to be, and to do what we are designed to do. We should use the present to impact our future. In difficult times, knowing what the future holds gives the strength we need to live our present well.

I began this chapter with the idea we are to love others as much as we love ourselves. Sometimes, we have misplaced love for ourselves. We feel the unmet personal needs associated with being known and loved, and we cannot give ourselves away to others. We may be confused about what our real needs are as we spin our wheels trying to feel good. Just as a hungry child often chooses candy over a healthy, satisfying, hearty meal, adults choose to be known about and liked rather than experience the real thing. It is very hard on relationships. We must seek to know the truth about ourselves, our design and purpose, and our real needs. Then, we will have the ability to make the right choices and do what is best for both ourselves and for others.

People naturally start with their personal interests and get stuck in self-seeking relationships. God has provided a way to move beyond that point. He has covered our sins. He has made relationship possible with Him. We can know Him and can choose to love Him. In relationship with God, we can truly know ourselves and experience the satisfaction, inner peace, and contentment flowing from our relationship with Him. It is an amazing and satisfying feeling knowing we are deeply loved, and knowing how valued we are by God. In that understanding, the love we have for ourselves will not be misplaced. Moreover, past relational hurts need not entrap us in chains of fear. We will find the ability to choose to know others, because they are worth knowing. We will find freedom to connect to them in order to meet their needs, and love them in truth rather than a relationship as a means to meet our needs. We will find freedom from fear of the future, and the pressure to manipulate relationships out of that fear. Freedom from emptiness and longing to be loved will provide the ability to make balanced choices in life each day. We will pay attention to our health and to our limits, understanding when we need to restore ourselves with rest, and when to expend ourselves for others. We will find the freedom to give to others in confidence and strength rather than take from them. We will be empowered as we to seek to know them, and to love them. We will find joy in living according to our design. Our life will be a blessing to everyone around, and we will be wonderful reflectors of our loving God.

DAVE COLLINS

13

KNOWING & LOVING OTHERS

We began our journey talking about the centrality of relationships in our lives. We talked about the two key elements of strong relationships, believing we are known and we are loved. We have discovered it all begins with knowing and loving God. Knowing and loving God allows us to know ourselves, and helps prevent us from working out of a self- serving kind of love. We have seen the risk associated with being known and loved by others, and how we tend to play games with one another in order to avoid the risks. We pervert truly allowing others to know us, as we substitute being known about for being known. Furthermore, we avoid the risk of loving, and being rejected, by seeking to be liked. We become people pleasers rather than lovers. All these games lead us to a roller coaster ride in relationships, as each of us takes our turn in the game. Few of us really find the depth we are looking for with friends, and even in our families.

We have seen God understands what we are doing and why. We understand He truly knows us and loves us wildly, enough to die for us. He has provided a way for us to escape the game, live a life filled with the joy of knowing and loving others, and having them know and love us. He has offered us freedom from our fears, and shows us how we can have legitimate needs to be known and loved met in Him. He has the answer for all our needs if we go to Him. Our inner emptiness can be filled and replaced with an inner peace in Him.

It all begins as we honestly recognize God is near. We begin to realize He wants to be known. He has revealed Himself in the universe He created. He has revealed Himself through men, and through the Bible. He has put on human flesh, and revealed Himself as one of us. He has told us all we need to know to live a great life. As we understand who He is, and walk with Him committed to go where He leads, a whole new life opens itself up to us.

Our relationships in life open up as we recognize we do not need to depend on others to give us value or for them to affirm we are worth loving. Consequently, we find freedom to treat everyone authentically. God has demonstrated He considers us beautiful and wonderful. We need not measure up to anyone else's standards. We have met God's standards. God has given us a new place, a new identity, and a new model for life. We do not have to measure up to our family's expectations, our friend's expectations or even what our culture considers right. God has given us a most noble plan for life exceeding anything we might otherwise try to live up to. He has given us the power to live that noble life. We can freely offer what others need, because God has already met our needs. We can face possible personal rejection, knowing the truth about who we are in Christ. It will still hurt, but the sting will not be strong enough to prevent us from loving anyway.

Knowing Christ also helps us know ourselves. Self-knowledge is more than being content with our physical make-up, our likes and dislikes, or our personality. There is also the understanding of purpose. We know we have talents and gifts, and they are useful, adding fulfillment to life. We understand part of life is discovering where we can serve best, learning how to give ourselves away to others employing all our talents, gifts, and personality. Everything has meaning and every person has meaning. Knowing Christ gives us freedom to live without fear of living a wasted life.

Knowing fullness and contentment in Christ is a powerful thing. It is power strong enough to calm anxious hearts, and transform self- absorbed people to ones who give to others freely. It is the power that enabled Alex to quit trying to fix Anna and simply love her. It gave him the power to stay with her and never give up. It is the power that enabled Anna to face her disease and do what it takes to control it and overcome it. It is the power in Christ that enabled Anne Sullivan to give everything a wild frustrated little girl needed to find life and the ability to connect to others. It is the amazing power of Christ that allowed five men to die by the hands of a strange people they only met days before. That power enabled a sister and a wife live with the same people who had killed a brother and a husband. They sought to know the people, their language, their customs. They shared their own lives and became known as kinsmen. They loved the people, and by the powerful love they shared with Christ, they saved an entire tribe from making itself extinct through vendetta killing. Love changed their culture completely.

This kind of love enables one to suffer for the good of others, or to right a wrong. It is the same power that changed me from an insecure, self-doubting young man, stumbling through life, to one who lives life with purpose and joy. Instead of fearing what people may say about me, I can let them see the real me. I have an honest desire to know them, and I have a noble desire to love them.

The power of being known and loved by God can transform anyone. You can experience new life with this understanding. God does know you. He loves you. He wants you to know yourself and understand how to live as you were created to live. He can empower you to let others know you and love you. He can empower you to know and love them. That is His desire. There is no greater way to live life. It will lead to deep joy, because life truly does center in relationships. As relationships become more and more authentic, the experiences with others will be deeper and more profoundly fulfilling. The memories experienced with others will be rich, and there will be a depth to life reaching farther and deeper than mere experiences can provide. A life filled with deep relationships is a life fully lived.

Life filled with authentic relationships does not come instantly. If you have ever tried to break a habit, you know how hard it can be. Whatever our age, we all start life's journey not knowing God. Until we know Him, we float through life trying to figure it out, carried along by our culture's currents, or living according to whatever conclusions we have drawn along the way. The consequences and paradigms built over years do not simply go away. It takes a lifetime to retrain our mind and our heart. Life truly is a journey.

One of those old tendencies that may stubbornly resist change is the belief we can manipulate people in relationships to get what we want. We think if we love people, they will love us back in just the way we want. It does not work that way. For instance, have you ever noticed young people who are starved for love, and live with that expectation? They want a girlfriend or boyfriend so badly they fall all over themselves to get attention. When they enter a group, tension begins to mount. People feel pressured and uncomfortable, and everyone feels awkward not knowing how to act. The starved person is trying too hard not realizing love does not happen that way. Love cannot be forced or manipulated. If we seek it, we miss it, but if we give it freely, it comes to us freely. This is how we are to live. We must freely give ourselves away without expectations of what we will get back from others. Then, we will be surprised at how freely we will feel known and loved in unexpected ways.

As we set out to know and love God and the people around us, it may be helpful to have a few ideas about how to go about the task. What can we do to know someone deeply? How can we begin to practice loving? Here are a few ideas to get started. Understand that we are all different. As a man, I think like a man. Some of these ideas may come across that way. We also have different personalities impacting how we act. The important thing is to change our mindset from self to others, and to work at being transparent to make it possible for others to know the real you.

Knowing Others

1. Start with the most basic, often overlooked, indication that someone is known. Learn their name. I struggle remembering names, especially as I get older. I have to work hard to learn names and remember them. It is worth the effort. Have you ever felt the disappointment of talking with someone who should know your name, yet does not know it? We often offer grace to those people, but we do remember they forgot. On the other side, do you feel great when someone you have only met once calls you by your name? Again, our names are important, for they are part of our identity, and it gives us a sense of importance when people remember.

2. Play together. Even as adults, there is something about laughing and playing together that helps us connect. My grandchildren always want me to get on the floor with them and roughhouse. The boys love to wrestle and push me around. It may be the physical contact that is important, but playing together is a shared experience. It is through shared experiences we see into each other's lives. We know what we like, and dislike, and we gain insight into personality.

3. Find areas of common interest. We mainly find common interests through conversation. It can be a common cause. It may be hobbies or activities. When you find common ground, you have a place to connect and things to talk about. You have a way to share excitement and joy. When both parties are interested in the subject or the activity, there is the opportunity to be real and transparent.

4. Try to enter their world. When I was on Young Life Staff, I spent a great deal of time at the local high school. I was not trying to relive my past. Rather, I was entering the world of high school students. They knew I cared about them, and wanted to be around them. It gave me access to their lives. I could earn their trust, and was allowed to know what was going on in their lives. I am working to enter the world of my pre-school grandchildren now. I do that by asking them about things going on in their day. I show interest in their activities, and talk with them about things that excite them. It is not about teaching them or giving direction or advice. I simply try to hear their hearts to know what they are excited about, discouraged about, what they want to do, or want to experience.

5. Invite others into your world. This principle was demonstrated in one of the most amazing stories shared by a friend of mine in Young Life. He tells people today one of his greatest days was the time I invited him to come over to help me build a fence in my back yard. The invitation communicated to him that I trusted him. It made him feel welcome and accepted. He felt I valued his companionship, and it thrilled him that I wanted him around. We built a fence together, but it opened the gate for us to share deeply about our lives. This shared experience was very significant in both our lives. It happened over 30 years ago, and our relationship is still very close. At the time, I had absolutely

no clue about the impact our time together nailing a few boards together was having on his life. I simply wanted to be with him, and have his help doing life.

6. Talk. Men, particularly, struggle with this. We are so single focused and "fix it" oriented, that our conversation tends to center on the facts at hand. What needs to be done? What are the details we need? What is expected of me? We find it hard to talk about how things are impacting us. Feelings are usually acted out more than talked about. In conversation, we tend to analyze what is being said and work on our answer or comment before the other person is finished speaking. With our wives, we men tend to offer solutions to perceived problems before affirming the feelings going on inside their souls. More than likely, they are more interested in our understanding than in our solution. We must learn how to ask questions. We should not only seek to understand what is happening in the lives of others, but encourage them to share how they feel about whatever the subject is. We should honestly be interested in discovering who they are, how they feel, what is important to them. Ask yourself, "what do I want to know about this person?" Focus on them before offering your own opinions.

7. We all need to learn the art of listening. We should listen twice as much as we speak. If we really care about someone, we will want to understand what he or she is saying. Listen well enough to have follow-up questions. Help them clarify their thoughts by telling you more.

8. Spend time together. We cannot help but know someone with whom we spend time. Our culture is an instant culture. The social media communication tools serve a purpose. We get information quickly. But they rob us of time together and the opportunity to know one another. There is no such thing as instant intimacy.

Loving Others

We described love as caring enough about another person to place a high priority on meeting the needs of that person, as we are able. In the effort to connect to others, much of what we do to know them will actually feel like love. As we spend time and work to know them, listen to them, and share our lives with them, we are communicating our belief in their dignity and value. They will know we have chosen to be with them, and have given our time and our inner selves to the relationship. That in itself is loving. There are other things we can do to communicate our love for others.

1. We can take the initiative in the relationship. Do not always wait for others to call. Make the first move, especially when seeking to reconcile or resolve conflict. Do not be afraid to be the first to ask forgiveness or say, "I'm sorry." Often, life can get in the way of relationships. We must take the initiative to maintain contact with others. We can make the first move in a positive sense. Be the first to invite a neighbor to a meal. Make the first contact with someone you would like to know.

2. Let people know you appreciate them. Tell them when they have done something nice for you. Recognize when they have given time, energy, or support of any kind. Never assume they know you recognized their effort. Tell them, and remove all doubt. Appreciation includes the offer of praise for work well done, accomplishment, or strength of character. I find it easier to be around and listen to people who praise than to be around people who are critical. Praise and appreciation affirm our value.

3. Forgive, and do not keep score. There may be some who take advantage of you, but mostly people feel blessed by the gracious gift of forgiveness. True forgiveness is a gift with no strings attached. The other side of this coin is to ask

forgiveness when you have wronged someone. In asking forgiveness, do not explain why you acted as you did or make any excuse. Admit the wrong and ask for pardon.

4. Offer encouragement. It demonstrates you understand them, you believe in them, and you stand behind them. People who encourage others are fun to be around and build a sense of wellbeing.

5. Do something fun for no reason or special occasion. Invite friends to dinner or take them dinner. Leave a surprise gift. Show up to help with a task you know your friend has to do one day. Offer to baby sit to give friends a special night out. Be creative. Make it fun.

6. Touch appropriately. We discussed earlier the importance of physical touch to infants. It remains important throughout life. It comforts. It encourages. It communicates love in many ways. A simple touch around the shoulders or pat on the back communicates volumes. For married couples the absence of touch is a clear signal there are problems in the relationship.

7. Meet a need you know exists. To do this, you will need to have communicated enough to know the need. When you offer help, it is a way of saying you are committed to the one served. It says you care about them. It speaks to their value. If the help you offer is sacrificial, it communicates very clearly, by the depth of your sacrifice, the depth of your love for that person.

8. Learn their love language, and speak it. (Read The Five Love Languages by Gary Smalley) Each of us, due to life experiences or personality, is touched more deeply by one action or experience over another. For some touch is most important. For others it is receiving a gift. When we know a

person's love language, we can choose to do things that will shout our love to him or her. Consider yourself. Remember the times you felt loved and cared for by someone. What were they doing? They were probably speaking your love language. What we like, we tend to do for those to whom we want to express love. It is key to realize they may have a different love language than us. We will love more effectively if we speak their language. Work to know them deeply. Work to know their love language rather than simply do what makes you feel loved. We love when we choose to do what makes a person feel loved the most.

9. Share your soul with people. Generally, we men do not do very well with this. We talk about facts and can talk about any number of subjects. We find it hard to share our hearts. People feel trusted, and honored, when they can see more of whom we really are. What are you excited about? What are your goals? What have you been reading, learning, or studying? Be open about feelings, desires, disappointments, and the feelings and motivations that move you.

I have shared a few ideas about how to grow closer to the people around us. Recognize these suggestions may be a starting place for you. We all have blind spots that tend to sabotage us at inopportune moments. Being aware we have blind spots, seeking to uncover those little areas of weakness and actively working to get better are all part of the process of maturing in relational skills. We need to maintain open minds and hearts. We must pay attention to the people around us trying to recognize if they are not open to share themselves with us. If they are closed, we should ask ourselves a few tough questions. Have we failed to earn their trust? Are we trying to do things for them in order to get things from them? Do we really want deep relationships? We all sense when someone is not sincere or is trying to get something from us. We may be blind to our own selfish actions.

Love is a choice. My old selfish nature raises its head often in the sticky area of relationships. Sometimes I choose to take the easy route. Rather than spend energy to love, I will occasionally withdraw. I, like you, must choose what is important every day. I still need to discover old paradigms that hold me back. I need to learn and practice love. We must recognize the importance of our present actions, and abandon false beliefs from our past. Keep your eye on the fact your present relationships impact your eternal relationships. Remember, we have a lifetime to work on these issues. Tomorrow starts today.

Conclusion

At the end of our life, we may be remembered for great accomplishments or skills we have developed. We may have accumulated great wealth and goods. We may have served our company, our country, or the world in a memorable way. In the end, those things will not matter if we have done them alone. Life will have been lonely and dry. We will not have reflected our Creator accurately. We have all been designed to do great things in community with others. By God's design, we are meant to know others and be known. We are meant to love and know the fulfillment of being loved by others. It all begins with our Creator. He has made Himself known, so we can love Him. He wants to be intimately involved in our lives. In relationship with Him, we will discover peace within ourselves and joy in sharing our life with others.

May you have the strength and confidence to be who you have been designed to be. May you do wonderful things in your life. May you be free to seek out others, and may you want to know them. May you not be timid about revealing yourself to them. May you find deep satisfaction in loving relationships. Be courageous. Go for it.

NOTES

Scripture taken from the HOLY BIBLE, NEW INTERNATIONAL VERSION. Copyright 1973, 1978, 1984 International Bible Society. Used by permission of Zondervan Bible Publishers.

Scripture taken from the NEW AMERICAN STANDARD BIBLE, Copyright 1960, 1962, 1963, 1968, 1971, 1972, 1973, 1975, 1977, 1995 by the Lockman Foundation. Used by permission.

Chapter 1

1. Pet Rock has a trademark. U.S. trademark registration 76656255

Chapter 2

1. James Dobson is a psychologist who has written a great deal about children, families and family issues. He founded Focus on the Family ministries and continues to provide valuable input in childrearing practices. One of his early works provides great insight. Dobson, Dr. James, Hide or Seek, Old Tappan: Fleming H. Revell, 1971.

Chapter 3

1. Larry Crabb has documented biblical insights into counseling principles and philosophies. He has made significant impacts in counseling practices among Christian counselors. The basics of his counseling methods are found in Basic Principles of Biblical Counseling.
Crabb, Larry, Basic Principles of Biblical Counseling, Grand Rapids: Zondervan, 1975.

2. Paula shared thoughts about her grandmother in her book Gift of the Red Bird. D'Arcy, Paula, Gift of the Red Bird, New York: Crossroad Publishing, 1996, pp. 65, 66

Chapter 4

1. Shakespeare, William, The Complete Works of William Shakespeare, London: Abbey Library.

2. There were several letters exchanged between O.J. and Nicole Simpson. Many are in public records and others are on file in the trial records.

3. Jokes abound about marriage. I noted some in the Chicago Tribune.
Royko, Mike, Chicago Tribune, Chicago: August 19, 1993
Boyle, Lara Flynn, Chicago Tribune, Chicago: December 26, 1993

4. Paul Brand is most famous for his work with people who had contracted Leprosy. He studied the true nature of the disease and made observations about our body and its function based on his studies. I would recommend two of his books to gain deeper insight into how we naturally care for ourselves.

Brand, Dr. Paul & Yancy, Philip, Pain The Gift Nobody Wants, New York: Harper Collins, 1993

Brand, Dr. Paul & Yancy, Philip, Fearfully and Wonderfully Made, Grand Rapids, Zondervan, 1980

Chapter 5

1. Helen's story is told in her Autobiography, The Story of My Life. That story was put on film in 1962 in a movie

called The Miracle Worker. The film captures the frustration Helen felt, the difficulty her parents had in disciplining the unruly child, and the determination and persistence of Anne to help Helen understand. Some of their journal notes can be found in The Book of Virtues.
    Keller, Helen, The Story of My Life: with her letters 1887-1901, Nabu Press, 2011
Bennett, William J., The Book of Virtues, New York: Touchstone, 1996, pp. 312-317

2. The Waorani people are also known as the Huaorani. The spelling accepted by the them is Waorani. They are also known as the Aucas, a name given by the Quichua, descendants of the Incas. It means naked savage and includes a connotation of cannibalism.

The story of the Waorani can be found in several books and movies. Through Gates of Splendor and The Savage my Kinsman are accounts written by Elizabeth Elliott. Several books have been converted to documentaries called Through Gates of Splendor and Beyond the Gates of Splendor. The actual participants in the killing are interviewed in the movies as well as the wives of the five men who were killed. These are very powerful stories of the people who lived them and their children who followed. For understanding from the Waorani point of view, I recommend Gentle Savage. It is an account by three of the men who speared the missionaries and later turned to Christ.
Regarding the transformation of this tribe, we must recognize that to say, "the killing stopped" is a relative term. Anthropologically, this tribe did something overnight. They were at the point of exterminating their culture, and within a very few years completely changed their way of dealing with conflict. They still experience occasional spearings, but they do not live it as a way of life.

Elliot, Elizabeth, Through Gates of Splendor, Wheaton, Tyndale Press, 1956

Elliot, Elizabeth, The Savage My Kinsman, Harper and Row, 1961
Aenkaedi, Menkaye, Gentle Savage, Xulon Press, 2013.

Chapter 6
1. What's Forever For has been sung by many people. It was written by Rafe Van Hoy.
Van Hoy, Rafe, What's forever for, Sony/ATV Tree publishing

Chapter 8

1. Dallas Willard gives a thorough account of our heart condition in his book, Renovation of the Heart. He explains the human problem and the consequences of a lost heart.
Willard, Dallas, Renovation of the Heart, Colorado Springs: Navpress, 2002.

ABOUT THE AUTHOR

Following graduation from The University of Houston in 1972, Dave married his college sweetheart, Sharon, and began his career as a football coach in Houston. He discovered his heart was to influence young men's lives as a friend rather than as an authority figure. He joined the Young Life staff. After 13 years in Houston, he directed Young Life Austin and later served in Costa Rica 5 years. After 29 years, Dave left Young Life to minister to businessmen through The Gathering of Men. Currently he acts as a mentor to men in Texas and serves as a mentor and friend to missionaries in Latin America through Kingdom Calling Ministries. His family is his joy. Each grandchild has him wrapped around his or her fingers. His kids, Kayla and Aaron, learned how to do that at a young age and are now passing that skill on to their spouses. Dave loves to play golf and even finds he encourages his playing partners, because almost everyone beats him. Dave is an artist and loves to paint God's creation. God's creativity and beauty enthrall him and inspire him as an artist. You can see his work at www.davecollinsart.com.